Am I Bipolar or Waking Up?

www.bipolarORwakingUP.com

Am I BIPOLAR or Waking Up?

A Memoir by

Sean Blackwell

2011

All mental disorders carry a damaging stigma in our society. As a result, some names and locations have been changed in order to protect the privacy of family, friends and co-workers.

This book has been self-published with the help of Kindle Direct Publishing.

Cover Art by Oz J. Thomas.

ISBN: 9798373175845

Printed in the United States of America

To those of you who have been stamped

Your time will come.

CONTENTS

CAUTION

This memoir tells my story and reflects my opinions at the time the events took place. Those opinions have evolved somewhat and will continue to evolve over time.

In no way does this book give medical advice or make suggestions, one way or another, regarding medications for any mental disorder or spiritual experience.

If you are exploring alternatives to the mainstream psychiatric system, please do so carefully and with the full support of people who empathize with your struggle.

PROLOGUE

"Toronto police officers taking me to Heaven? This is hilarious." At least that's what I was thinking while being escorted to the Windsor Hotel elevator on a stretcher. I can still remember the feeling of those metal handcuffs digging into my wrists.

Freedom.

So free, I was sure I had died.

But the path to Heaven was much more difficult than I'd imagined. I had done everything possible to get there. I'd stripped naked, tried to push myself through a concrete floor, knocked on all of the ballroom doors, even tried to turn out the lights of the hotel! That's when the cops grabbed me.

For reasons beyond my understanding, Wellesley Psychiatric Emergency was to be the vehicle of my journey. Once restrained to a bed, the entire hospital felt like a spaceship sailing through the cosmos. Luckily, my father had come along for the ride.

I was never able to look at myself or my world in the same way after this most improbable of life defining moments. In a single weekend, not only my identity, but all of my dreams and ambitions were completely destroyed.

Thank God for that!

The life waiting for me was much more interesting than the one I was leaving behind. My previously monotonous routine quickly morphed into a mission of adventure and intensity. Where I had once buckled under the demands of "the real world," I now stood tall, confronting life's challenges with a soulful defiance.

It took an entire decade to discover that my spiritual awakening was much more common than I had imagined, and that those who are blessed by the experience are usually diagnosed with bipolar disorder. Once that happens, a lifetime of medication is not so far away.

After finding that out, my mission became clear. I needed to speak up and start sharing my story. I needed to let everyone who would listen know that what may look like a *break-down*, may also lead to a *break-through*.

So I'll let you be the judge:

Am I Bipolar or Waking Up?

Part 1

Rude Awakening

HANDCUFFED

JANUARY, 1996

"If you're so smart, why aren't you happy?"

It sounds like an easy question, but as I stared into the bathroom mirror of my Vancouver apartment, it was one I was unable to answer. Despite being out of university for six years I still hadn't managed to get into a fruitful career stream. No matter how hard I tried to make things happen, opportunity simply refused to knock. My life had become a prison cell out of which there was no escape.

And I had escaped. Or at least I thought I had. I'd moved as far from my old life as I possibly could – 3,000 miles! Yet, the same issues, *the same people*, would follow me all the way from my hometown of Toronto to the Pacific Coast.

Before I left Toronto I swore to myself that I would never go back to a media job in an advertising agency again, and yet there I was, working for the exact same agency, OMNI Advertising. Why? More money, of course, and maybe the chance to earn a little respect.

However, what started out as promising soon turned disastrous and, once again, I found myself in a desperate career situation – a career that I hated. I was starting to wonder if I would ever be as happy as I was in the first effortless nineteen years of my life.

Finally, one night, a year and a half after moving out to Vancouver, I picked up the phone to share my grief with my ex-girlfriend, Carmen. I was expecting a normal reaction from her which would have been to tell me to "get off my ass!" Instead, all she said was, "Sean, take The Forum."

For six months Carmen had been encouraging me to take this strange course she said had changed her life – The Landmark Forum. This time I agreed to look into it. I think it was the tone of her voice that convinced me. Something was there that I'd never heard from her before. Compassion. Was it The Forum that gave this to her? Maybe.

What the hell, I had nothing to lose.

A few days later I went to an introductory seminar, where people interested in taking The Forum sit in with about thirty "graduates" who have moved on to the "commitment" seminars. I was taken aback by the openness and sincerity of everyone – perfect strangers sharing their deepest insecurities with each other; all there because they felt some level of failure, sadness or dissatisfaction with their lives. These people were taking personal responsibility for transforming their lives for the better, at least for the moment.

I thought, "Even if I don't get anything out of it, whatever happens to these people on The Forum weekend must be interesting to watch." I got curious.

Then, two smiling, middle-aged ladies took me in for the hard sell.

"Why are you here?" they asked me.

"I feel completely handcuffed," I told them. "It's as if, career-wise, I just can't get a break and I don't know what to do!"

After we discussed my frustrations for a while they asked if I wanted to register for the next seminar. I told them that I wanted to "wait and see" because I wasn't sure if I was going to stay in Vancouver. The agency had just put me on probation after a dismal and raise-less review. Fearing unemployment, I thought I might need to move back home if I lost my job. They assured me that if I were to move to Toronto, I could re-book my seminar with Landmark's Toronto operation.

"Do you know what happens when you 'wait and see?'" one of them asked, rhetorically.

"You wait…and see."

She was right. I signed.

After registering, these two volunteers were so happy I thought the program must be some sort of con.

"We just love seeing people take the first steps toward putting their lives together," they said.

"You'll be surprised. It's as if, as soon as you sign up for The Forum, it's working for you!"

"Sure," I thought.

The next day was another gorgeous January morning in Vancouver. Strolling to work from my brand new condominium (that I rented with two other guys), I was feeling much better than I had during the past few months.

On the way, I was talking to myself: "You know you love this place. You also know that from moving here with nothing last year, you will survive, even if you're fired at work. The hell with advertising! You can just stay and sell mutual funds or something."

At that moment, I decided to permanently live in Vancouver and resign from OMNI, ending my career.

Except, a funny thing happened.

As soon as I arrived at work, my boss ushered me straight into her office.

"Annette called from Toronto," she said.

My ship had come in.

Annette Jones was the former head of account planning at OMNI Vancouver. Account planning was the hottest field in advertising and had been so for the previous decade. In a nutshell, the role of the planner involves conducting qualitative research (usually focus groups or in-depth interviews) in order to arrive at a richer understanding of how consumers relate to the brands they buy. They then help translate that understanding into compelling advertising strategy. Good account planners were highly respected and made big bucks. In addition, along with "creatives" they were the only agency people that could get Green Card status to work in the United States – a dream I'd had since high school. I was always thinking about how I was going to get over that border and out of the cold.

Despite hating my job in the media department (which involved the mind-numbing task of buying advertising air-time on television and radio), the only career I could ever envision for myself was account planning. As soon as I'd heard of the profession, three years earlier, I knew I would be terrific at the job and, eventually, a remarkable success story – if I could just catch a break.

I'd already applied for account planning positions on three different occasions with OMNI. Each time I got closer than I thought I would, but was rejected in a more embarrassing manner.

News of the last rejection was communicated to me by the most junior person in the entire agency, a twenty year-old media assistant, while we were at the local pub. He knew they had hired someone else for the position before I did.

However, this time was different. I could feel it. A year earlier, I'd volunteered to do some on-the-street interviews to help the agency prepare for a big client presentation. It was then that I was able to get my foot in the door with Annette Jones as a possible junior planner down the road. Unfortunately, she left the company before I could jump-ship from my own private media nightmare.

Over the previous few months I'd occasionally been in contact with her regarding possible openings at the tiny three person consultancy she was working for in Toronto, WeCU Creative Planning. This time, she was calling to tell me to send in my resume. Apparently, the owner of WeCU was thinking about hiring one more junior account planner.

Three days after receiving Annette's call I decided to move back to Toronto and put everything I could into getting that job.

Those middle-aged ladies at Landmark Education were wiser than I'd thought. *It was as if The Forum had started working for me already.* From the day I got that call, my time in Vancouver felt like the night before Christmas.

So now you know why I took The Landmark Forum in the first place. The only reason I signed up was that I felt completely stifled in my career. In fact, with the exception of my job, life out West had been quite the ride.

From the minute I arrived, I had a surprising number of friends and an enviable social life. I was physically active in a way that was impossible in Toronto – skiing, roller-blading, even scuba diving on a few occasions. Plus, the agency handed out a lot of free tickets for events around town, so it wasn't like I was at home, miserable.

However, the biggest improvement came in my spiritual development. My time in Vancouver was a period of transition, when I began to see God back in my life again. The "miracle" of Annette Jones calling on the same day that I decided to walk away from my advertising career was just one in a long series of *synchronicities* I'd experienced out West – absolutely impossible coincidences which I recognized but did not understand.

How I came to this spiritual transition is a story in itself. So, before I tell you what happens next, let's take a step back…way back.

GOD-LESS

Growing up in the 1970s and '80s, religion was always a big part of my life. Baptized at birth into the Roman Catholic Church, Mom had me and my brother, Glen, bussed out of our mostly Protestant neighborhood to a Catholic grade school a few miles away. Catholic high school was even further! As a family, we *never* missed church on Sunday, not even during the NFL playoffs. I prayed almost every night and even read The Bible. No, not parts of it – the whole thing, cover to cover. About one page a night for five years. Seriously.

Enrolling at The University of Toronto, however, my focus became more critical as I began to painfully absorb ideas that conflicted with my own faith. In economics and sociology it was Karl Marx's mantra, "Religion is the opium of the people!" which my professors recited. Over in the psychology department, Freud had everyone believing that religion was a symptom of human weakness. "God is dead!" cried Nietzsche, the philosopher, and we killed him. I'm still not sure how that happened. Then, in religious studies, I discovered an entire range of religions – some believing in thousands of gods, then others with no god at all!

Needless to say, I graduated a little confused in the God department.

Eighteen months after getting my B.A., I started my first "real job" as a media assistant at OMNI Toronto. By that time, God was the last thing on my mind. Basically, we just stopped speaking to each other. But was He/She/It even there at all? I had no idea. You could say I became a closet agnostic.

To be honest, I just didn't care anymore. I was too busy struggling to build a career at the height of Toronto's worst recession ever, than to follow up on the spiritual questions which remained unanswered. Mind you, without God I wasn't getting very far. During my first two years at OMNI Toronto I was actually earning less money than when I was in high school, working at the local supermarket (when you worked it out by the hour).

They were, without a doubt, the most difficult years of my life. I had accepted a position right at the bottom of the agency food chain with the expectation that, by proving myself, I would work my way up quickly. Instead, I got labeled a "media guy," and a pretty average one at that. As the boredom and disappointment of my newfound career sunk in, I started making some serious errors, the kind that get you noticed by the suits upstairs – in the wrong way. Once that happens, you can kiss your career goodbye.

During those godless years, the only person to rekindle my interest in religion was theologian Joseph Campbell, whom I discovered in a series of PBS interviews with Bill Moyers.[1] Riveted by the ideas this man had to share, I watched all six hours of those videotapes three times. I remember vividly, wishing that I could see life as he did, but it was simply impossible. Campbell's world of divine inspiration was as far removed from my harsh, mediocre reality as could possibly be.

Somewhere on the journey from high school to university to the world of advertising, life had lost its magic. The whole process of studying your life away until entering the workforce, where you are supposed to work your life away, appeared to be totally meaningless, especially where I was employed. Despite my best efforts, the most meaningful work I could imagine for myself was *advertising?* While rationally, I thought I had potential in the field, it just seemed to be a part of the problem, not part of the solution. But what was the solution? I had no idea.

Back then, all I knew was that I was so struck by the meaninglessness of my life that I would find myself crying in movies…a lot. Like, the movie's over, the lights are up, people are leaving the theatre and I'm still in my seat, crying my eyes out. Like, now I'm out in the parking lot, sitting in my car, still crying.

Not…normal.

Why was I crying? The movies inspired me. The characters were bold and heroic in their actions. They threw themselves into the fire, stood up for the right thing, the hell with the consequences. And where was I?

In my cubicle checking contracts.

I did make a number of attempts at getting better positions, both inside and outside of the company, but it was no use. I was stuck. It was as if everyone around me could sense my despair, and wanted no part of it.

"Quit! Quit that fucking OMNI!" Carmen used to shout at me. But, following the age-old logic of, "Don't quit a job until you have a new one," I continued to hang on.

"Why do you need to have everything so planned all the time?" Carmen once asked me. "Why can't you just…take a chance?!" I had no reply.

It was a slow and gradual slide, but after working in advertising for just over two years, I found myself at the bottom of my first true depression. On my twenty-eighth birthday, March 27, 1994, I felt so lifeless that I called in sick. I had nothing left.

A few weeks later came my yearly performance appraisal. I went into the meeting thinking that if they didn't give me at least a $3,000 raise, I would quit. My unhappiness was no great revelation to my boss. After criticizing me for having an attitude problem, she offered $2,000.

I walked out of the meeting relieved that she had made my decision so easy. I went back to my apartment with a bottle of wine for a sad, lonely celebration. It was finally over. I had just wasted two years of my life.

Little did I know, there would be one more loss that night. At the time, Carmen and I were sharing a tiny studio apartment downtown. A few days earlier, she had returned from a month-long trip to India. From the moment she walked through the door I could see that she couldn't look me in the eyes, but I was so numb by that point, I chose to let it go.

This night, however, I was ready for the truth. Going to bed, it came out of me in such a matter-of-fact way, "This is over, right? You don't want to be with me anymore, right?"

At first she was reluctant to respond, but eventually she confessed. After Carmen shared a range of clichéd excuses as to why, I turned over and went to sleep.

"Now I can go to Vancouver," was my only thought.

The next morning I awoke feeling, well, *unusual.* My girlfriend of three years had just broken up with me and I was about to quit my job and face unemployment.

"I'm a twenty-eight year-old failure," I thought.

"Why do I feel so good?"

Deep down, I knew why. I'd wanted to move out West for a few years, but commitments to my job and Carmen had kept that dream on ice. Now, nothing was holding me back.

Arriving at work the next day, I met with my boss and gave her eight weeks notice – enough time to make arrangements, move back home and save some money.

My depression was over. So was my agnosticism.

SYNCHRONICITY

The day I resigned from OMNI Toronto, I did have one particular concern. If I moved to Vancouver, where would I stay? My only contacts out there were two people I'd partied with years earlier. Already aware of their circumstances, I knew that staying with either of them was impossible. A few weeks in a hotel would leave me with no money at all. Who could possibly put me up? It's a good thing I had some photocopying to do.

Rick, my former supervisor, was standing over the copier as I waited for him to finish.

"Sean, I just wanted to let you know that I'm leaving the agency and moving back home to Vancouver," he said.

My search was over before I'd even gone to lunch.

By the end of the day, I was getting a little suspicious about what exactly was happening to me, "First the job, then Carmen, now I already have a place to stay?"

My suspicions continued.

With the exception of my first week at OMNI Toronto, I always had a mountain of contracts, invoices and estimates to sift through at my workstation. Although they all looked like paper, they acted more like boomerangs, as every time I tried to get one of those little nightmares off my desk, it would somehow find its way back. But, by the end of the week, they were simply vanishing. A phone call here, an e-mail there, and poof! Gone.

Despite absolutely no change in my responsibilities, my last eight weeks at work were a dream. If my job had been that easy for the previous two years, I never would have quit!

It felt as if life itself were orchestrating my departure.

Two months later, I packed my '88 Mazda hatchback with my life's belongings and hit the road. I thought I'd be mostly bored by the ride, but each day brought with it unique delights.

Day One I visited a guy from Windsor, Ontario whom I'd worked with for a few months. He'd left OMNI to open a jet-ski rental shop on Lake St. Clair. He had me up on one in no time! Jet skiing at sunset was the last thing I expected to be doing my first day on the road.

Day Two was a quick visit to Chicago. With its many modern skyscrapers, it was a lot bigger than I had imagined. Day Four was Mt. Rushmore, South Dakota. That was a little smaller. I actually preferred the giant dinosaur at Wall Drug – more of a surprise, I suppose.

Day Six, near Calgary, I went to my first country hoedown with another ex-OMNI guy and a bunch of his yahoo cowboy buddies. Day Seven I drove through the Canadian Rockies with a hangover – *bad idea.*

Each day of my solitary journey carried with it a greater feeling of lightness. Colors brightened. The air smelled better. The stomach pains that had been bothering me in Toronto disappeared. I had nothing to go to, but yet, I was filled with energy and optimism. It felt like the whole world was opening itself up to me.

The sight of Vancouver knocked me out. I'd heard it was beautiful, but not like this. Framed by blue-green, snowcapped mountains on one side, and the Pacific Ocean on the other, it was love at first sight.

Before I even got to Rick's place, I called my parents from a pay phone.

"I believe in God again!" I told them.

Before leaving Toronto, I'd become quite thoughtful about the style of life I would like to have in my new existence. Being a bit of a TV addict, I wanted to experiment with living without television. I wanted to get back in shape and start eating better. I wanted to earn $28,000 a year, which may not sound like much, but it was $6,000 more than I was making in Toronto. Besides, it matched my age.

After having back-to-back girlfriends for six years, I wanted to actively socialize with people of my own choosing, instead of being filtered into hanging out with *their friends*. Plus, I wanted a nice place to live, even if I had to share it with a roommate.

There was also one more subtle choice. I wanted to be less cynical. Sure, the world was full of problems, and perhaps life had not given me a fair shake recently, but I came to see how focusing on everything that was wrong in the world, everything that was wrong in my life, just didn't help the situation. For some people, I think I'd become a bit of a downer to be around. With the move, I chose to let that cynical side of myself go.

Within two months of arriving on the West Coast, everything had fallen into place. I was sharing a newly renovated house two blocks from the ocean. I started lifting weights four nights a week. The few friends I had out there were thrilled to see me and, before I knew it, my social life was packed. As for the television, I never touched it or a newspaper. If the world was coming to an end, someone would fill me in.

I was positively giddy with how fast it all came together. So giddy, in fact, that I started to see how what had happened to me seemed almost *dreamlike* – that the reality in which I was currently living was first created *in my mind*.

There was one small exception. As I mentioned earlier, I did swear to myself that I would never go back to a media job. Yet, from the day I moved in with Rick, the temptation was there. Little did I know, not only had Rick returned to OMNI's Vancouver office, but our director, Mark Jacobs, had moved from Toronto to Vancouver as well. Apparently, I had started an exodus!

It's a long story, but political shifts in Toronto had alienated both Rick and Mark. As they had worked together in Vancouver a few years earlier with great success, they both decided to return and help rehabilitate an office that had fallen into disarray. At first it was Rick telling me how short-handed they were, and that I should give it a second chance. It wouldn't be long before Mark would be calling as well.

Mark was the one who originally hired me in Toronto. Knowing how frustrated I'd been there, his first offer was for me to come in on a freelance basis, until I found a full-time job elsewhere. As I was quickly approaching the end of my $3,000 savings, it was a tough offer to resist.

OMNI Vancouver was in such a beautiful location – a converted warehouse overlooking the harbor, with a funky brew-pub on the main floor. I even had my own office! Although I was just a freelancer, it felt like a huge step up from the "Dilbert" lifestyle I'd endured in Toronto. Those first few months were very special.

Soon, Mark approached me with an offer for a full-time position at the money I'd envisioned for myself. In retro-spect, I think he thought I'd been short-changed in Toronto and wanted to make it up to me.

It was a difficult decision, but as I had nothing else lined up and things had gone so well, I chose to return to the one company, the one job, that I swore I would never return to.

One August evening, I was having dinner with *another* recent ex-pat from back home. I'd met Junior through Carmen, back when we were all doing a lot of clubbing together. A struggling actor, he'd made the move to Vancouver to see if he could jump-start his film career.

Over drinks, I told him about my terrific new circum-stances and positive outlook on life. We also talked about the stunning coincidences that had guided me to where I found myself losing my job and Carmen on the same day.

We even discussed the "coincidence" of us having dinner together on the other side of the continent when, four months earlier, neither one of us was planning a move. "What a coincidence!" Junior shouted, with a half-drunk belly laugh. By then, the humor of the moment was obvious as we realized that these were not "coincidences" at all.

We also spoke of other ideas I'd recently pondered, which came to me during the long silences of my eight-day drive.

"I realized that when I like someone, it's because I like the way *I feel about myself* when I am with them," I told him. "But, with people I don't like, what bothers me most is how *I feel and act* when they are around. In truth, it's not them I dislike, it's me! It is as if there is no true Sean, but a Sean-Junior, a Sean-Carmen, a Sean-Rick. I'm different, depending on the *energy* I feel with the person."

The most pressing example I had was of an old friend from grade school who I would constantly argue with over Canadian politics. With other people, I rarely argued over anything, and I never talked about politics, as the subject bored me to tears. Yet, with him, it was the same irritating conversation over and over. Why?

"You know, I'm reading a book that covers a lot of what you are talking about," Junior said. "Maybe you should pick it up. It's called *The Celestine Prophesy*."

The following evening I called Carmen in Toronto. We had remained friends and talked regularly after our break-up. I told her that I was beginning to piece together a new perspective on the way I think the world operates, and that it is completely different from how we had been taught.

I told her of how Junior and I had discussed these ideas the night before, and that he had recommended a book.

"Oh my God, *The Celestine Prophesy!*" she exclaimed.

"That's right," I said. "How did you know?"

Carmen was reading it as well, and had been blown away by it.

I told her how I thought the world *really worked* – that we are not exactly individuals, but all sort of connected and that coincidences or *synchronicities* play a critical role. The conversation lasted two hours (back when a long distance call was expensive). Without prompting from Carmen, I talked about the different aspects of my new perspective and, inadvertently, covered the first six of nine "Insights" discussed in *The Celestine Prophesy*.[2]

"Sean, that's the Fifth Insight!" she whispered in excitement.

The next day I bought the book and read it in two nights. Everything I'd been thinking about was there, spelled out clearly in Insights One through Six. I was flabbergasted.

After that, I started reading a variety of spiritual books, all the while becoming more and more introspective. I created more quiet time for myself. I also got my birth chart done by an astrologer that I met, by "coincidence," in a Mr. Submarine sandwich shop. I had never met an astrologer before, and yet, just when I was in the market for a reading, there he was, going over his charts in the middle of a fast-food restaurant – not something you see every day! I still remember his last words to me after my reading, "Sean, you're a king and you're gonna live for 100 years!" I guess it could have been worse.

In order to help me with my spiritual development, the astrologer recommended the works of Dr. Carl Jung. In his biography, *Memories, Dreams, Reflections*, Dr. Jung goes into detail regarding important dreams he had and how they helped him guide his life.[3] Inspired by his approach, my dream world became much more vivid than it had ever been. I started giving my dreams extra attention, deciphering their symbolism whenever possible.

One spiritual subject led to another, as I eventually picked up my first books on astrology, Buddhism and a few New Age philosophers, just for kicks. I also returned to literature on Taoism, a philosophy that had intrigued me since university.[4]

My passion for studying these subjects arose from genuine curiosity, but it was also motivated by one troubling anxiety. The move out West had gone amazingly well, but I didn't know why. This ignorance on my part left me feeling insecure. I needed to get to the bottom of it.

Over the Christmas holidays, I had an ominous dream which suggested that my newfound success may not last:

> I was sent to Spain on a business trip, flying the plane of Charles Lindberg, *The Spirit of St. Louis*. I could see myself flying over the Atlantic Ocean in his open-air cockpit. Arriving in Spain, I landed on a dusty, rural airstrip. Two farmers took my plane into the hangar, while I went into the city on business.

When I woke up, I asked myself, "Charles Lindberg? Why him? Why his plane?" Then it hit me.

After Lindberg crossed the Atlantic, he was so famous that he became a target for criminals. At one point his baby was kidnapped and never returned.

Charles Lindberg lost his baby.

"That's it!" I thought. "I'm afraid of losing my baby, but my baby is me – this new, optimistic Sean that has grown out of years of depression. I'm afraid of losing the new me."

For better or for worse, this dream would have a profound impact on my life.

One day, I was having lunch with *another* friend of mine from Toronto, Sandy, who worked near my office. I told him about the Lindberg dream and how, through the dream analysis I was learning from Jung's biography, I was opening myself to new insights regarding my life.

Then I said to him, "But it's not like the symbols in one dream mean the same thing for everyone. For example, suppose we both had exactly the same dream which, of course, would be impossible – but just suppose. If I dream about a tree, it may mean something completely different to me than if you had seen a tree in your dream."

Up until that point, Sandy had seemed rather skeptical and, perhaps, bored with my new understanding – but then the miraculous happened.

"I had a weird dream the other night," he said. "I dreamt that I was in a cabin in the middle of a valley, surrounded by trees. Near the trees were these deer, and they came and attacked me. I was attacked by deer in the woods."

I was dumbfounded.

My new roommate, whom Sandy had never met, shared with me the same dream a month earlier! Eventually, I got them together for drinks and they both had a correction to make from their dreams. The deer had horns. In fact, both had not dreamt of deer, but of elk. I suspected that maybe I was the attacking elk, that my new ideas were somehow threatening to both of them.

Weeks later, I shared this synchronicity with the astrologer, who had an interesting perspective on the whole thing. Over coffee and a donut, he informed me that he suffered from schizophrenia. Back in the 1970s, during one of his episodes, he hijacked an airplane with a toy gun in order to "end the Vietnam War." While he was in jail for this crime, his cellmate gave him a book, *Black Elk Speaks*. Based on my story, the first thing my new friend did was recommend that I read this book as well. It is the auto-biography of Black Elk, a Lakota chief and shaman. *Black Elk Speaks* would be my first book on the subject of Native American shamanism.[5]

I found all of these mystical connections to be very meaningful and inspiring. The spiritual opening they created left me feeling as if life were one gigantic adventure, where one astonishing discovery only leads to the doors of countless others. However, on the negative side, it seemed the prophesy of the Charles Lindberg dream would come to full fruition. I was about to lose my baby.

Over the course of January – June 1995, my status at work went from company hero to company zero. I slowly came to realize that I was not going to enjoy this stint in media any more than I did at OMNI Toronto. My main client contact, a brand manager for X&Y Restaurants, had a well deserved reputation as being a bitch from hell. Due to my inexperience on her business and being painfully over-worked, she quickly lost faith in me, as I did myself.

To make matters worse, a girl had joined my department just before Christmas who I quickly fell in love with. As a result, I just couldn't concentrate at my desk.

"I'm in love, but I'm not ready!" I told myself. But it was too late. Everything was falling apart.

By the summer of 1995, I'd been officially taken off the X&Y account at the request of the client and the girl I was in love with wouldn't even speak to me. Out of despair, I was having sex with the eighteen year-old office receptionist. I was twenty-nine at the time. My life was a mess.

Over the next few months I was able to piece back together some sense of dignity. By September, the girl I was "seeing" dumped me for another guy in the office. I got the woman I was in love with speaking to me again, and my director, Mark, put me back on the X&Y account, giving some stern words to the client who was ruining my life. I got some redemption.

While life did become somewhat lighter, my career still stagnated. And, as I mentioned earlier, the account planning job that I missed out on was a huge disappointment. So, by the time I got Annette's phone call about the junior account planner position at WeCU in Toronto, I felt as if my life in Vancouver had taken me to Heaven, Hell, and everywhere in-between – *but it all seemed to be for a divine purpose.*

DEATH

Before leaving Vancouver, I decided to transform my last few weeks into a bit of a celebration – a farewell tour, if you will. After work, I was out at the bars with friends and co-workers as often as possible. I caught rappers, Cypress Hill, De La Soul, as well as bassist Bootsy Collins, all while they were in town. I even shared NBA tickets to the now defunct Vancouver Grizzlies with that girl I was in love with and her homely new boyfriend. Better to make peace, I suppose.

My most memorable farewell was one final SCUBA diving expedition with my friend, Owen. A diver with the Canadian Navy, he was the reason I got my SCUBA certification while I was out there. Owen was the experienced "dive buddy" I could trust. I'd called him to say that I was moving back to Toronto and was wondering if we would get a chance to go on another dive together. As it turns out, he had planned a "wreck diving" weekend in mid-February, a month before I was leaving. Everything was clicking again. I signed on.

"Owen, I know it sounds kinda sick," I said, "But, if you were gonna die, a wreck dive would be a pretty cool way to go."

"Don't even say that, Sean," he replied, in a foreboding tone.

Owen and I shared a ship with about fifteen other experienced divers, the owner and his wife. The boat itself had a certain machismo to it – big, cold and ugly. Perfect.

The next morning I awoke to find our ship at the dive site, just off the pristine coast of Vancouver Island. The B.C. Reef Society had sunk an old Canadian destroyer out there. It was sitting on the sea floor at 130 feet. The deck was at about 90 feet. Being a novice diver, I was only supposed to dive to 60 feet, but I felt comfortable going deeper with Owen by my side.

I wasn't planning on doing any major penetration of the sunken destroyer, because that would be too dangerous for me to try, but I thought I might swim through a door, here or there.

Our initial dive went off without a hitch. While the ocean was ice cold and disturbingly dark, visiting the bathroom of a military destroyer at 90 feet below sea level is a memory I will never forget.

I did have a small problem with my weight belt, though. The high water pressure at that depth was squeezing my wetsuit, causing the belt to slip. By the time I surfaced, all of the lead weights on the belt had slid around from my hips to my abdomen.

On the second dive we went down with the owner of the tour boat. Together, we had agreed to do an easy penetration of the upper deck of the ship. That was the plan, but I had a cold feeling about this guy. His beard was too long.

This time, I grabbed a different weight belt and tightened it as best I could before our descent, positioning the weights on my hips in a way that would avoid slippage.

As we descended along the dive line, the murky water limited our visibility to only about ten feet. The current had picked up considerably as well. It was a little hairy.

After arriving on the destroyer's deck with Owen, we waited for the owner and his dive buddy to follow. But instead of following the plan, the owner waved us to the front of the ship, down below deck. We were descending below 90 feet now, a depth that I wasn't comfortable with. The owner then pointed to a three-foot wide black hole in the front of the ship that he wanted us to enter – for me, the equivalent of suicide.

As I floated there, waiting for the group to make a decision, my weight belt slipped. I grabbed it and tried to pull it tight. But as these belts are designed for quick release in case of emergency, that's exactly what happened.

I went shooting to the surface as my weight belt slipped off my legs and down to the sea floor. Since we had only been below for a few minutes, I knew my chances of getting the bends were minimal, but if I didn't slow my ascension speed, relax and exhale, I could die instantly from a brain embolism.

I did all the right things. I emptied my buoyancy control device of air, relaxed, exhaled and spread out like a starfish to slow my ascension. I remember reaching for my depth gauge at twenty-five feet, where water pressure begins to decrease rapidly, wondering if I was going to die.

It was a cool feeling.

I hit the surface with Owen just a few seconds behind. He'd heard my high pitched murmuring as soon as my belt dropped. Embarrassed by my rookie mistake and pissed off that I'd lost the belt, I wasn't even thinking about how close I'd come to death – but everyone else was.

Once I got back to the ship, the looks of concern from the other divers jarred me. I didn't realize the finality of what could have happened until I saw it in their eyes and heard it in their voices as they asked me if I was "okay."

I went to bed early that night, a little shaken, but in a way I wasn't familiar with. I had nightmares about our ship sinking, filling with water as I lay in bed, helpless.

So, with this and a myriad of other memorable experiences to take home with me, I returned to Toronto for my quest to finally land the job of my dreams.

LIFE

Two weeks before my thirtieth birthday, I took a meandering route home through the Oregon desert, Idaho and Southern Wyoming. Engulfed by all of the ancient red rock down there, I began to think of the possibility that perhaps all of this is a dream.

"Maybe my soul isn't moving across the country, but just thinks it's moving because my mind has senses that tell it so – *just maybe.*" My exodus to Vancouver had meant the fulfillment of many dreams, and many nightmares as well.

I returned to Toronto in preparation for quite a week. I'd set up an initial job interview with my potential employer, David Stone, for Thursday. I was able to land an interview with him, not because he was dazzled with my resume – far from it. It was my method of delivery that did the trick.

Back in Vancouver, I'd Fed-Exed him my resume to arrive before Valentine's Day, with a Valentine card telling him how much I loved "His Agency." Inside the card was a Top Ten List of reasons he should hire me. Reason # 6 was,

"I enjoy being beaten and verbally abused by my employer (if you're in the mood)." Reason #1 was, "Everyone else sucks!"

It turns out the guy had a sense of humor. I was in.

Funny enough, I was able to transfer to a Landmark Forum Seminar in Toronto, which started the following day. Like I said, things were clicking. However, by now, my reason for going to The Forum was a little different from my original intention.

I first signed up for The Forum because I felt "hand-cuffed." Now that a genuine career opportunity had presented itself, I wanted to see if I could help myself avoid the pitfalls that I might walk into out of ignorance, fear, or most importantly, stupidity.

I wanted that job with WeCU so much that I drove back across the country just for the first interview. But there was never anything that I'd wanted this badly that I'd actually gotten. This time, I didn't want to blow it.

The Thursday of the interview, things went surprisingly smooth. David was a tall British planner who oozed an almost absurd amount of confidence. I sensed that we immediately liked each other, but I also knew that he wasn't going to commit to a "media guy" with no account planning experience without careful consideration. That first interview was just the beginning.

The next day, The Forum started at 8:00 a.m. My first impression of the seminar was the implausibility of what their staff said would happen. With 150 of us sitting in a fairly tight seminar room, the idea of any life changing moments occurring seemed far-fetched. After all, people spend years in one-on-one therapy sessions without experiencing any profound changes in their lives. How could one solitary speaker create true breakthroughs for so many people in a single weekend?

The atmosphere was one of cautious anticipation, as none of us were sure of what to expect. There was a little bit of nervous small talk in the room, as if we were waiting for a university lecture to begin.

We had been greeted and seated by what I later learned were Landmark volunteers. They were nice, but had an overly nice way about them. Then again, maybe that was just me being paranoid. The guys had a lot of facial scars, like they were ex-drug addicts or gang members. It all seemed a little cult-like.

When the session began, up came this petite woman who looked like an attractive version of Margaret Thatcher. I can't remember her real name, but she was bold, charismatic, articulate, and very, very funny.

The first thing Thatcher did was address any concerns members of the group had regarding the nature of the course and, most importantly, some of the unusual rules they insisted we promise to follow. These rules were put in place, she said, because previous experience had shown that they help to make the seminar a much more effective tool in impacting everyone in the room. Many people had a problem with this.

The rules were as follows:

- No going to the bathroom until the set breaks, which were about every two hours.
- The normal class day went from 9:00 a.m. until almost midnight. Nobody was to leave early.

- We were all obliged to arrive on time with homework assignments completed.
- No talking or whispering during the lecture, except when we were instructed to break out into pairs for discussion.
- We were to stand up when speaking to the group leader.
- We all needed to be there because we wanted to be there; not because we were pushed into attending by a boss or loved one.
- That we were all basically normal people lead- ing normal, healthy lives, functioning adequately in society:
  "This course is very psychologically stressful. If you have some sort of psychological disability, illness, or are in therapy you should not take this course."

This last part was already reinforced by the waiver they had us sign before we registered. Having never even visited a therapist, I signed without hesitation.

It took *four hours* for everyone to agree to all of the rules, and to ensure that they were all there voluntarily. This delay occurred largely because of challenges to the rules by some of the older men. There were a few guys, over fifty and set in their ways, that were sent to the course by their wives and didn't like being told when they could and could not go to the bathroom.

For every one of these challenges, Thatcher met the complainers head on, refusing to let them sit in quiet resig- nation. She forced them to either willingly say they would comply with the rules and spirit of the program or leave.

One guy took over twenty minutes. Her ability to confront these headstrong men was impressive.

Another guy was chronically depressed and had tried to kill himself a number of times. Thatcher discouraged him from taking the course and asked him to seriously think about why he wanted to participate. After the break, she asked him, in front of the class, if he was going to stay or leave. This guy had been in therapy for years. He decided to stay. It was a moving experience for everyone in the room, and we hadn't even begun.

Once we were into the program, a lot of the ideas introduced were familiar to me from my readings on Taoism and Zen Buddhism. The first concept they asked us to "try on" was the notion that there is no such thing as a real, objective, factual *interpretation* of reality. That yes, something happens in the physical world, (e.g., a man kissing a woman), but the meaning we automatically attach to that event which we also think of as "reality" is simply our perception (e.g., is the kiss romantic? Vulgar? Immoral?). It is a valid perception because it is one that reflects our life of experience and learning, but it is only one possibility among a myriad of perceptions. It is not "objective reality."

Now, you may already know this, and so did I at that point in my development, but many others didn't so we had to spend a lot of time on this idea.

Later, Thatcher talked about how our perceptions get us into arguments, and how it is the nature of humans to defend their point-of-view at the expense of relationships – that we would rather fight, righteously defending our perceptions and values than "love" each other.

She then got us to define ourselves by listing our values, which led me to reflect on arguments I'd had in the past. I recalled Nietzsche writing about how every nation has a different set of values, and that these are the things, more than anything else, that they are prepared to go to war over. As individuals, people are the same way.

I instantly understood what Thatcher was getting at and felt humbled by my ignorance. I'd never considered how harsh and unfeeling I must have seemed to people when I was convinced that I was right and they were wrong.

It was my friend, Wendy, that initially came to mind. Wendy was not the most rational person in the world. One day we had an argument over which direction we were heading in my car. I said we were going north, she insisted we were heading west. I eventually realized that the reason we were arguing was that, while I knew we were heading toward the geographical North Shore of Vancouver, we were on West Georgia Avenue. The fact is, we were going northwest. When I explained this to Wendy she still laughed at me, insisting we were heading due west.

To settle the argument, I pulled into a gas station to buy a map, graphically proving that I was correct. Although the map clearly showed that we were heading northwest, Wendy still would not admit it. With conclusive proof in hand, her refusal to concede defeat pissed me off. I became cold and argumentative. She was hurt and caved in. "Hooray!" I won the argument, but had damaged our relationship, all over which way was west.

Everything they taught at The Forum sort of sunk in like that – right away. They were taking concepts I knew were correct, intellectually, but forcing me to apply them to my own life. While others in the course often appeared confused or skeptical of what they were learning, I was absorbing everything like a sponge. It all made perfect sense.

The first day was about how we define ourselves in this world. We were asked to look back on the exact moment when we decided that our definition was appropriate for us. Then we reflected on how these definitions were the very things that were causing conflicts in all of our relationships with others.

Boom!

This was an insight of staggering proportions to me – that my definition of myself as being intelligent, individualistic, and honest to a fault, were actually limiting my relationships with co-workers, family and friends. I was also able to look back into my childhood and see the exact moment I started unconsciously defining myself in that manner.

I could apply these and other insights to my own life in a way that created within me a sense of startling revelation. By the end of the first day I felt like I'd gotten my money's worth out of the entire course.

Arriving home that night, excited beyond belief, I found my parents talking with my brother, Glen.

"So, what did you learn today?" my dad asked in his typically interested, but teasing tone.

"I'm an asshole!" I replied, ecstatically.

Naturally, they disagreed. "Well, you're not an asshole," they said.

But then I went on to explain what I meant. That I finally understood how my unconscious arrogance with people made them feel bad about themselves when I got into arguments with them, and that regardless of what the discussion or argument is about, keeping the relationship open and loving is much more important than being right, being the "winner," or preserving the integrity of my ego.

My parents listened patiently, but they were cautious about my tone. I was talking a mile-a-minute and they were a little lost as to what exactly I was talking about. Glen had a better grasp of what I was trying to say.

Before I went to bed, I had a request for my dad.

"The Forum asked that I bring someone on Tuesday night (the last night of the course) that I think would benefit from the course. So I thought I'd ask you tonight, *before I go really nuts.*"

I was alluding to the fact that my parents were not keen on me taking the course due to its cost (about $300) and its "cult like" qualities (the long days). I asked Dad on the first night because, if I became even more excited as the weekend went on, I might become filled with so much zeal as to make him think I truly had joined a cult!

All of this was a big joke in the family.

When friends or relatives asked what I was up to that weekend, Dad would say, "Sean's gone off to join a cult." Yes, Dad was enjoying his digs, but I knew he'd come, even if he thought it was all bullshit. Mother, on the other hand, wouldn't be caught within ten miles of the place.

We were assigned homework that night, but it was homework I didn't do. They wanted us to think of the person in our life that we were the most estranged from or had the most conflict with, and write him or her a letter of reconciliation. The letters would be shared at the beginning of the next day.

I went to bed that night wondering who my letter should go to. I just didn't feel like I had any relationships that were in need of mending. Many people at The Forum were trying to recover from serious issues such as divorce, death, strokes and alcoholism. By comparison, my problems were not only small, but non-existent. I had a happy home life, good relationships and I liked myself. I just wanted a job!

Saturday morning was the first time people had the opportunity to open up and tell the rest of us why they were there. They would do this by reading their letter to a partner they were sitting next to or, if they felt like it, they could stand up and share it with the rest of the class.

Thatcher had warned us the night before of how most of our letters would probably sound. She said that many people, while desperately wanting to heal an important relationship, would end up blaming the other person for everything bad that had happened between them. She was expecting letters like, "Dear Dad, I love you very much, and I'm sorry for getting angry when you start acting like such an insensitive jerk."

A few people were asked to voluntarily read their letters to the rest of the group. I didn't think there would be much of a response. Who would want to read such a personal letter to 150 people?

I was wrong.

Hands were up all over the place. It became obvious to me how much pain a lot of these people were in; how badly they wanted to get their lives in order and their relationships healed.

Thatcher selected the first person to get up and read his letter. The guy stood up,

"Dad..." was the only word he could get out before he broke down in tears. His letter was not what Thatcher had anticipated. No blame, no guilt, no defensiveness. This guy just wanted his dad back in his life.

One after another, people stood up with a different, tragic scenario, but the same desire. People had had enough of trying to hold their high and mighty lives together. The people in this room (most of them anyway) had given up.

They had surrendered.

After hearing from about six people, the one transsexual in the room stood up. A lot of tears had been shed by that point in the morning. But instead of reading his letter, he began to sing,

"Feelings...nothing more than feelings..."

The whole room cracked up. Then he read his letter.

"Dear Mom, I'm writing to you from The Landmark Forum course I told you about. If you remember, one of the reasons I wanted to take the course was so that I could be around normal people. But now I'm wondering if there is such a thing."

That became the theme of the weekend for me. As Thatcher said, "The only difference between regular people and the crazy homeless folks you see on the street is that their lips are moving."

At the break there were phones out in the hall so that we could make calls to the loved ones with whom we were in conflict, to begin the healing process right away.

But during the breaks I wasn't on the phone, I was on the toilet.

Every single break I had to go to the men's room to relieve the worst intestinal gas I'd ever had. I was there, every two hours for three days. As I wasn't eating anything unusual, I became convinced that there was some mysterious relationship between what I was learning and these non-stop runs to the bathroom.

It was as if the gas was connected to old experiences, stored in my intestines, which were now leaving my body because they were no longer needed. It seemed that I was, quite literally, letting go of the past.

Many different concepts were thrown at us on Saturday and Sunday. Thatcher talked about how people rarely listen to one another because they *already think they know* what the other is going to say, "Already Always Listening" they called it. She then discussed how the personality traits we use when life is going well are our "Winning Formula," and those traits we resort to when life becomes difficult are our "Losing Formula." She also showed us what we get out of being the "victim" in our relationships, and how that lets us avoid taking responsibility for our own lives because being the victim gets us love and sympathy from others.

Then, most importantly, she talked about the root of all this destructive behavior, which is fear – not fear of what we are currently experiencing, but fear of what might happen in the future, because of what has happened in the past. As a result, our focus is not where it should be, which is how we are living in *the present moment.*

She's talking Buddhism – and I'm buying it.

By this point, she had me. I was in tune with everything coming out of Thatcher's mouth. But then something happened that was basically the turning point – where I went from interested, open-minded "normal guy," to a member of the "cosmic order."

"Now we are going to feel our fear," she commanded.

"You are in a very safe space and it is perfectly fine to feel this way."

She then had us close our eyes, lower our heads and focus on the thought that, "Everyone in the room is trying to attack you…everyone wants to harm you."

She shouted out that scenario, or ones similar, repeatedly. I found it all rather lame. These people were among the meekest I'd ever met. I wasn't the least bit afraid or intimidated by anyone in the room. As a matter of fact, I couldn't recall ever being afraid. I was always a pretty brave guy. I stood up for myself in the school yard. I played tackle football. I was even pretty good at public speaking. Is anything scarier than that?

I thought I was fearless.

Then I saw the scuba depth gauge at twenty-five feet. I felt a force puncture my chest like a fist. It entered at my solar plexus and rose up through my body to my head, forcing me to burst into tears out of nowhere.

I didn't know what had happened, but I was feeling fear now. I let the memory of my diving accident blend into thoughts of being taken hostage, of being surrounded by terrorists. Hunched over, with my knees quivering, I was thoroughly immersed in the experience. Yet, at the same time, I was completely aware that this was not actually happening – that it was all in my imagination.

Or was it?

"I could be an actor," I thought to myself. My tears were real.

I wasn't the only one. People were sobbing, throughout the room. One guy screamed as if he'd just met the devil.

With the tears, came another revelation:

"All my life I thought that I couldn't feel fear...that I was somehow different from every other human on the planet...I thought I was crazy!"

It was a tremendous relief to discover that, deep down, I was just like everyone else. As this thought passed through my mind, Thatcher changed directions.

"Follow your fear," she ordered.

"Follow it to the other side...there is something interesting waiting for you on the other side of your fear, something quite funny...follow your fear...."

"Does anything there appear to be absurd to you?" she probed.

I burst out laughing.

"Yes!" I thought. "Me! I am completely absurd. I am absurd!"

The sense of relief was overwhelming. Immediately, I thought of my father, the most absurd person I'd ever met.

It must have been earlier in the course when they had asked us to define our parents. When I thought of my mother, the only word that came to mind was "perfect." But when I thought of my father, nothing came to mind. To me, Dad was an indefinable entity, a living being beyond explanation; an impossible combination of walking, talking paradoxes that cannot possibly be fully understood.

He was, in every sense of the word, absurd – and that is why my love for him has always been unconditional. There was nothing he could do that would be beyond the mental boundaries I'd set up for him, because, by unconscious definition, my dad had always been indefinable.

For the first time, I truly understood the absurdity of my own life, and that of everyone else's. We are all logically impossible. In other words, we are all miracles; entities that never should have been able to happen; creatures that cannot rationally exist.

That's when I started to feel myself sort of slipping into the environment.

Swimming in a sea of bliss – overjoyed, ecstatic, shaking, and perhaps a touch crazy.

And, as much as I knew that my love for my father was unconditional, I could also see what many women had been telling me for years:

"Sean, you've got a problem with your mother."

"Sean, sometimes I don't know if it's you talking or your mother talking."

"Sean, have you been talking to your mother about us again? You have, haven't you? I can hear it in your voice."

For the first time, I could see my problem, *clearly.*

NEUROSIS

M om comes from a line of matriarchal families, where the men were largely unreliable and the women held everything together. My great grandmother, whom I never met, raised six kids in a marriage with a man who drank heavily, beating her and the kids along the way. The only story I ever heard about her was that she always told my great grandfather, "As soon as the last child moves out, I'm leaving you."

Back in the 1940s, women rarely left their husbands, even if they were total jerks. The day after her last child left home, my great grandmother packed her bags as well.

"I always respected her for that," Mom would say. Mom admired her for not leaving him, for the sake of the children, and then keeping her word and her dignity by following through with her own departure.

My grandmother was the same type of woman. The whole family called her "Mother Margaret" – even her own brothers and sisters. Because she came from such a large family, she was forced to forgo her education so that she could help her mother raise her younger siblings. Once she had a family of her own, Granddad was a little unreliable with the paychecks, so Mother Margaret was left to pay the bills, clean the house and raise four kids at a time when most women didn't work outside the home.

The day my grandmother died, the last two things she did before going to the hospital were lay out my grandfather's shirt and tie for him to wear to her funeral, and give him $26 to pay the phone bill when it came in at the end of the month.

I think by now you can understand the sort of lineage my mother comes from. She is a strong woman from a line of dependable matriarchs. And just like they did, man, did she rule the roost.

Now retired, Mom had been an executive assistant with a large Canadian corporation for many years. She went back to work after staying home to raise my brother and me into our late teens. After returning to the workforce three days a week, time and time again she would come home with performance appraisals recommending her for management positions, if she would only agree to commit to full-time status, which she was reluctant to do. Back then there was no real financial need for her to work at all.

In the '80s, Dad was raking it in, earning a six-figure income selling industrial real estate. The money was so good, my parents were flying off to The Bahamas for the *long weekend*. However, once free-trade kicked in with NAFTA, the industrial real estate market went down the tubes, as did my dad's career.

As a result, the '90s began with Mom working full-time, paying the mortgage, cooking the meals and cleaning the house – just like her mother did...and her mother's mother did.

The executives she worked for used to call her "The General."

Mind you, I was a powerful force in my own right.

Born under the sign of Aries, I was a true God of War. As a toddler, I took great pleasure in antagonizing those around me, especially my mother. I'd lock her out on the balcony; paint my bedroom walls with my own "personal" art supplies, located in my diapers. I slept sporadically, keeping my parents up all night with non-stop cries for attention. Most children have some curiosity regarding electrical outlets, but once they are shocked, that's the end of it. I would go back for more, hairpin in hand.

Like a lot of young boys, fun for me was hitting anything, but especially the private parts of my relatives. My earliest nickname was "Bulldozer" for the way I crawled across the room, creating havoc wherever I went. Later they called me "Baby Huey," after the big duck on TV that none of the other smaller ducks wanted to play with. I was simply too rough. The other kids my age scampered away in fear.

Early on, Mom figured out that if she didn't take charge, I would. This wasn't a battle that the General was about to lose. In retrospect, I think I was disciplined fairly, but often. Always warned twice before receiving punishment, I always had to take that third time just to see what would happen.

Whenever I see little kids running their parents' lives in a grocery store or restaurant, I think of the time I was spanked, pants down, in the meat department of the A&P supermarket. That's how they did it *old-school*. It may have been the late 1960s, but Mama was no flower child!

My behavior improved once I started kindergarten. I liked school and was good at it. It wasn't as boring as staying at home. I was pretty popular too. In first grade I had six girlfriends, or so I thought in my head.

Looking back, I think the discipline my mother instilled in me was necessary, although occasionally, I wasn't sure what it was for. Mom was the ultimate authority figure, the keeper of all information on what was good and bad, right or wrong. Because she never violated this strict moral code that only she knew, she took a place in my head as being "perfect."

She always knew where everything was. She never made a mistake. She trusted me and gave me a long leash in high school. Whenever I was yelled at I felt that, somehow, I deserved it. I think this is where the "neurosis" came in.

As I got older and needed to make my own decisions, her image of being "all-knowing" stayed with me. I would think about what I wanted to do, but her voice would always be there encouraging me to do the opposite. My dad reinforced this situation. His only rule in the house was, "Sean, your mother…" meaning, the only thing that I could do wrong, in my dad's eyes, was piss off my mother – not a difficult thing to do.

Planning my return home from Vancouver to pursue the WeCU job, I was haunted by two thoughts. First, I dreaded the non-stop dialogue with Mom about me forgetting advertising and going back to school to get my MBA. Although I'd considered it while I was in university, as time passed, I came to reject everything that an MBA represented. But Mom wouldn't let it go, always telling me about some "hip" young guy at the office that just got his MBA and now has a wonderful life.

My other worry involved an incident that happened a month before my return. I was driving home one night and, as I pulled into the driveway of my condo, I clipped a car that was illegally parked too close to the driveway. When I saw the dent in my car, the first thought that popped into my head was, "What's Mom going to say?" My gut cringed at the thought of her disapproval.

If I were seventeen years old, these feelings would be understandable, but I was about to turn thirty!

It was about that time that I considered the possibility that perhaps all of the women in my life had been on to something. I did have a problem with my mother.

I didn't see her as human, and her perfection made me feel inferior. All I could ever aspire to be was a person as good as she was. But being imperfect, I would never get there. In my mind, I just wasn't good enough.

Most of what I just wrote came to me during The Forum weekend. I hadn't really put it together until then. As with the "fear" exercise and realizing that I was an "asshole," understanding my relationship with my mother awakened me as never before. Imagine, all of this from a guy who just thought he needed a better job!

Driving home from the Forum that night, I thought I truly understood what it was to be human. On one level, it was the saddest story I'd ever heard, and on another, the most beautiful. Here we are, all us humans, gods stuck in the bodies of animals, all pretending to "have it together," busting our asses to fulfill some artificial image of who we are "supposed" to be – always wearing this brave face that everyone else can easily see through, if they care to look. Of course, we've been trained not to do that either. How many times do we truly look each other in the eyes? Not that often.

And here I sit with the answer. We don't need to put on the mask, because when we put on ours, others instinctively do the same. We are completely unaware that what we are protecting ourselves from is *an illusion*. And while the illusion will not kill us, the masks we use to make us feel strong and "good enough" will, because these are the things that ruin our relationships with others. Anything that separates us is a sin; anything that connects us is a virtue.

We are forced through the history of our cultures and families into a situation of constantly having to prove that we are "good enough" against some immeasurable, ever-changing criteria. Meanwhile, we are all fine, just the way we are.

If all of us could only grasp this simple idea, the world would change overnight. If every inch of us knew that we were more than okay, that the real us was God itself, there would be no reason for our fear-driven manipulations and defensive maneuvers. The illusion of money, status and power would disappear and we would all find Heaven on

Earth. When I would think of the magnitude of the universal neurosis I'd come to understand, I would weep.

What made the story even sadder was that to explain it to a normal, fear-driven person would be impossible. They would simply think you are crazy. You are standing right in front of them, experiencing the equivalent of Heaven on Earth, trying to help them understand, but they cannot believe you. They want to, but they just can't because they fear the unknown, part of which resides within them. They would rather toil in the mediocrity of day-to-day strife than risk the thought that life could be radically better than it is today.

By Saturday night, I was in one world, everyone else was in another.

Arriving home that night, my reality had transformed. In front of the bathroom mirror, I could hear the sound of my hair being combed. Staring at a towel on the rack, I immediately saw every fiber. Once in bed with the lights out, I was awestruck. The velvet black darkness blanketing me was the most beautiful thing I'd ever seen. It dawned on me that, as a child, you could "see" that darkness and were naturally afraid of what was lurking within it. Your mother would tell you, "Don't be afraid, there is nothing there," but the *nothing is something*. I could see the "nothing," the blackness, and it was beautiful.

My sleep didn't last long.

Nervous energy shook my entire body. I was awake at 4:00 a.m., frantically scribbling down my new insights in the kitchen. Mom got up from her sleep to see what I was doing.

I spilled my guts about how I had seen her as "perfect," but that was just the beginning of a confession of stuff she didn't know about.

Years earlier, a girlfriend of mine had an abortion. I made the call. I took responsibility so that she wouldn't have to. I carried that guilt with me for a long time. I carried a lot of guilt over past relationships. Guilt about not caring for a few girlfriends the way I should have. Guilt over leaving them. Guilt everywhere.

My last relationship was one where I tried to repent for previous sins. When we first met, Carmen was totally lost. But she knew it, and had a fire within her in which I could see potential. I made a decision to care for her like a father would a child; to give her the same sense of responsibility and values that my mom had given me; to raise a nineteen year-old girl as if she were my own. You scratch my neurosis, I'll scratch yours.

I gave Carmen everything I could while we were together, including the trust and freedom to go to India for a month without me. She returned the favor by having an affair with some guy in Bombay. Part of me was angry about that, but on another level, I felt like I'd finally gotten what I deserved.

I told Mom about that too – how I felt redeemed knowing that I had tried to help Carmen become a better person. I felt like I'd taken a life, but now had helped someone get theirs back. My relationship with Carmen allowed me to forgive myself.

It wasn't easy for Mom to hear, but I had to get it out. It felt like I was vomiting memories at her, explaining things the family could never have understood, because they were my secrets – secrets that separated them from me.

As the night of confession went on, I told her of how I felt like there had been a lack of affection in our relationship when I was young. Her hugs were always stiff and guarded.

"I want a hug!" I demanded. "A real hug."

She wrapped her arms around me in a warm, protective embrace. I needed it.

As we talked through the night, I could see how concerned she was. I also feared that, if she knew what I was actually thinking, she would think that I'd lost my mind.

"I don't think you are crazy," she insisted, trying to console me. She was really scared. She couldn't possibly understand what was happening to her boy.

WONDERLAND

I arrived at The Forum on Sunday feeling spectacular. I'd learned more about myself in the previous forty-eight hours than I had in the past twenty years!

For me, there wasn't a whole lot more to absorb. Thatcher might have introduced a few new concepts, but I felt as if none of it mattered anymore. It was more of a day to summarize what we had covered, where we were at, and where we could go with this newfound wisdom.

"Life is about nothing," Thatcher said, "…and because life is about nothing, anything is possible."

There was a bit of encouragement to get out there and live our dreams, the hell with the definitions and limitations. But, by this time, I was way ahead of her. I'd suspected that some sort of spiritual, synchronistic magic was running my life in Vancouver. Now I had proof.

That afternoon they asked us to call the person who had recommended the course to us so that they could attend the evening session. I called Carmen, who was happy to join me.

After the session, Carmen and I went for a drink to talk about my experience. I mentioned how I could see things now that I'd missed before, especially the darkness.

"Isn't it wild!" she said. "It's like you're on acid!"

I'd never taken acid (or any other drug), but from what I'd heard from others, the sensation was similar. Thatcher had warned us that this shift in perception could occur. "For some of you things may look very, very different," she said. "Not to worry, it will wear off in a day or two."

Returning home, feelings of wide-eyed optimism mixed with sadness over the state of mediocrity most people accept as simply normal life. Even though it was past midnight, I started calling friends in Vancouver who I thought could benefit from the course. I also told them how important they were to me. In retrospect, I certainly bit off more than I could chew, trying to save everyone from everything. They all listened quite openly, but were understandably cautious regarding my emotional intensity.

Waking up on Monday morning, I started to consider the possibility that maybe I was creating this whole scenario, everything around me, out of my own imagination. The wall separating fantasy and reality had begun to dissolve.

My parents and I would have long talks in the kitchen.

"Sean, we're concerned," they said. "You're very emotional and we don't like to see you like this."

"It's like I've been to Heaven and back, and you want me to act normally! Wouldn't you be emotional if you had been through that?" I replied.

As this was a day off from The Forum, I decided to go shopping. I wanted to buy some notebooks so that I could write down the insights and experiences I was going through. I was not in this world.

For the car ride, I grabbed a De La Soul cassette from our stereo cabinet. As I mentioned, I'd seen them in concert the week before I left Vancouver. It was a "goodbye night" with some of my closest friends. I'd seen many rap concerts in the past, but De La Soul's desire to ensure that all of us had a time to remember was inspiring. After the show, they stuck around to party with the crowd, hanging out near the dance floor. I approached Maceo, the D.J. of the group, and told him how much I enjoyed the show. We talked for a while. I felt a true connection.

Inserting their tape into my car stereo, I had them in the back of my mind from Vancouver. This time though, they sounded entirely different. Previously abstract, indecipherable lyrics were now crystal clear. The album begins with a song called The Daisy Age – a prophesy of a time of love on this planet that will begin "about five years from now." The album was five years old. It dawned on me that what they were talking about was a time when all of mankind would exist in the timeless state of mind I was experiencing at that precise moment.

More and more, my imagination and the "real" external world merged together. Entering Fairview Mall, I decided that, unlike an adult who walks from A to B, I would go where I "felt" like. For a long time I couldn't get out of Sears. Walking in circles doesn't get you very far.

Finally arriving in the atrium, I heard music over the mall speakers, I think. As I "wandered" through the mall, the song playing was "The Wanderer" by Fabian. I couldn't tell whether the music was coming from "out there" or from inside my own head.

I peered into the tiny display window of a jewelry shop where I found five watches. All of them had a second hand, except for the one in the middle. Testing reality, I tried to create a second-hand on that watch with my mind. I took another look and the second-hand which, apparently, wasn't there before, appeared. I recalled some of my readings from quantum physics, which said that time was an illusion, a mental construct. I gazed at those second-hands; telepathically commanding them to stop, then start, speed up and slow down. It was working!

Leaning against the corridor balcony, I raised my head to the skylight, feeling the warm sun on my face. I stood there for a long time, allowing the Divine to wash over me.

The sales people at Levi's seemed warmer and more sincere than the last time I was there. As I went to pay for a pair of jeans, I noticed a petite, Asian girl working the register. She tried to swipe my Visa card for the transaction, but it didn't work. She was getting frustrated, obviously insecure about keeping me waiting. After trying the other register, which stalled as well, she apologized.

"That's okay," I said to her.

"I can get money from the ATM and come back to pay with cash."

Instantly, she relaxed and the Visa card went through on the same register, which wasn't working a minute ago.

"It was very interesting meeting you," she said.

As I walked out the door, I felt a bit of a headache. It came when I thought of myself as being a particularly "good" person for the way I interacted with the cashier.

I then noticed that if I had a negative thought, the headache moved to my stomach. As the day went on, I got more of these stomachaches and headaches, only to realize that when I thought of myself as "nothing," not good or bad, did this energy center itself near my heart. That was where it seemed to belong. I felt as if my soul had been somehow unleashed, moving up and down throughout my body, depending on the tone of my thought patterns.

In one store, I saw a photo of a little boy on a board game. For five minutes I stared at him, trying to see if I could make him talk. He never did. It wasn't that I was sure he could, I was just experimenting with my newfound powers, testing the laws of physics in a world which was totally new to me.

I bought a T-shirt which reminded me of what I was learning at The Forum. It said, "If Assholes were Airplanes this Place would be an Airport." It was stupid, redneck humor, but it was appropriate. In an effort to protect our phony self-image, all of us act like assholes and don't even know it.

In fact, if we could understand how, why and when we act like that, the change in society would be miraculous. People wouldn't just be "nice" because it's polite. For the first time in history, we would actually *connect* with each other, all of the time.

To my astonishment, right there in the middle of the mall was a small petting zoo for children. I'd never seen it there, before or since. I stood at the fence, questioning the reality of what was in front of me.

All of the children were petting smaller animals, mostly goats, but in the back of the corral stood a solitary camel. I noticed that he was swaying back and forth, like large animals do when they are cooped up in a small space. Nobody was petting him because he was too big. I recalled how I'd been taught that you should be wary of camels because they are ornery and like to bite.

I thought about it for a few long minutes, and then entered – the only adult without children. I walked straight over to the camel. He made a grunting noise, acknowledging my presence. Imitating him, I grunted back. He swayed away. When he swayed back he grunted again, looking me straight in the eyes. I never wavered, grunting at him, mimicking his sound. He swayed away.

The next time he swayed back, he brushed his cheek against mine, and swayed away again. When he swayed back the next time he buried his head into my chest like a baby. I put my arms around him. I heard a woman behind me gasp at the affectionate gesture of the camel.

Our intimate interactions caught the attention of a few others – two llamas and a couple of executives had come up behind us. The zookeeper, who I'd been talking to earlier, came over as well.

"I know what it is to be on LSD," I told her.

"Are you on anything now?" she said.

"No, but I know how it works," I replied.

"It allows you to forget the thing you are trying to forget, but you don't even know you're trying to forget it."

After saying goodbye to the camel, I talked to the zookeeper for a while, telling her about the course I was taking, and then left. But after a few minutes, I returned to give her the address of where the final evening of The Forum would take place – The Windsor Hotel.

"If you're interested, I'd like you to come as a guest of mine. I think you'll get a lot out of it," I said.

"I'll think about it," she replied.

Afterwards, I sat down on a bench, feeling lost in a mall I'd been to hundreds of times before. Then I realized that I was not a child, like I'd pretended to be during my whole day there, but that I was an adult too, and could move linearly, asking for directions if I needed them.

Before leaving, I visited Grand & Toy Stationary to buy some hardcover notebooks in which to keep all of my writings, and then headed back to the car. Out in the parking lot I was, once again, over-riding my linear logic. I walked a number of steps to the middle of the lot and paused, waiting for my intuition to kick in. I felt an urge to look to the upper right of the lot. There was my car.

I can see how someone could easily interpret all I have written about my day as the goings-on of a man who has lost his mind. But I was functioning, talking to people, and happy. I knew I wasn't in our "normal" external reality, the one we have all been taught to see as the real world, but I was also uncertain of my experience being simply a figment of my imagination. I felt in-between those two states. I was confused, but it was a joyous confusion.

PURGATORY

The closing session of The Forum was held on Tuesday evening at the Windsor Hotel. Despite the fact that my parents had been dealing with a very flaky son the previous few days, Dad kept his word and came with me – sitting in the back row with his sunglasses still on. I was wearing my "Assholes in Airport" T-shirt.

The ballroom was packed with giddy graduates, and the people in their lives that they thought could most benefit from the course.

I scanned the room to see if the girl from the petting zoo came. I found her sitting in the middle, looking straight at me. I bolted over to her and quickly thanked her for coming, then rushed back to my seat.

I've forgotten most of what was said that night. Initially though, Thatcher asked some people to stand up and tell the others in the room what they had learned.

The first to stand was the guy who had read his letter to his father on Saturday morning. He'd brought just about his entire family. His dad looked just like him.

I was waving my hand frantically in the back of the room. Thatcher asked me for my name, but for some reason, I wouldn't tell her. I think I wanted it to be a mystery. She insisted, but I refused. As I got to the microphone I had my dad stand up, along with the girl from the petting zoo.

"I've learned that I'm as absurd as my father," I said. I don't think anyone in the room had any idea of what I was talking about.

"And this girl over here, I only met yesterday!" I proudly proclaimed.

I didn't get much of a response from the crowd. I'm not sure if they knew what to make of me, or what I'd just said.

At the break, the guests were asked to join the Landmark volunteers in separate rooms where, as I'd briefed my dad earlier, they'd be given a bit of a hard sell.

In the meantime, a woman I'd met at the seminar came over with the girl from the petting zoo. The woman gently explained to me that the girl was not from the zoo at all, but was her cousin! I asked the girl if she had a sister or any relative that looked like her that would have been working at Fairview Mall the day before. She said no. I asked her why, then, did she stand up? She replied that it was the pressure of me asking her to do so in public.

I'm a little more embarrassed now than I was then about what happened. I couldn't believe it. She looked just like the girl I'd met the day before, and she had looked right at me when I came into the ballroom. I started to think that, in response to my outlandish behavior, the Universe was playing a bit of a trick on me.

"Well, you still played an important role in my life!" I said to her. There were no hurt feelings or anything. They thought it was funny.

With my dad in getting the hard sell, I sat alone for the second half of the session. Thatcher proceeded to summarize much of what we had covered and how we could apply these lessons to our daily life.

Mesmerized by the magnificent chandeliers above us, I started to tune out. I realized that I had already received all of the answers to all of the questions I thought I would ever need to know.

"My God," I thought to myself, "This is the kind of information I thought I would get only when I was dead."

Then it hit me.

"That's it! I'm dead! I died during the diving accident, and this is some sort of Purgatory!" I thought to myself.

I then realized I'd been dead for a month and hadn't been aware of it. But, because I was undergoing this mysterious "Purgatory adjustment process," *everybody* must be in on it!

"None of us here are human," I thought. "I'm dead and everyone around me is some type of angel."

"Everyone knows I'm dead, but me! This is all an act!"

I laughed hysterically at the profoundness of this cosmic joke. Every acquaintance, gas station attendant, Forum volunteer and member of my family knew that I was dead, but acted as if I were alive in order for me to learn what I needed in this "in-between" world. After being sufficiently educated, I could move on to Heaven (or wherever it was that I was supposed to go). And who was going to tell me the truth? Nobody, because everybody was in on it!

As I was arriving at these enlightening conclusions, Thatcher was at the front asking people where their heads were at regarding what they had learned over the weekend. She asked people to raise their hands if they were stuck on certain points she had talked about. If you raised your hand, she would recommend, tongue-in-cheek, that you sign up for the advanced Forum course.

I just sat and waited for her to finish. There was no reason to pay attention now, as I knew my time in this Purgatory was coming to a close. My father had done his job and quietly exited.

Concluding her lecture, Thatcher said something that stuck with me, "If you haven't raised your hand yet, you don't need to take the advanced course. Feel free to proceed through the Valley of Death."

The crowd laughed at her last line. I wasn't laughing. It was the first thing I'd taken seriously all night.

I picked up my coat and wandered toward the door. I was on my way to Heaven, but then paused as I wasn't sure which way to go. I simply stood against the wall, waiting for guidance.

A Forum volunteer approached me.

"Excuse me, I'm looking for the Valley of Death?" I asked, in a rather comical tone.

She sent me over to the opposite corner of the ballroom. By this time, I'd put my name tag on upside down. In the corner was another volunteer. I'd met this guy a few days earlier. I'd talked to him because he looked like a magician from television – Penn, from the team Penn & Teller.

It hit me as soon as I went over to him, he didn't just look like a magician, *he was a magician*. This guy was somehow connected to this elaborate joke regarding my death.

"Hi," I said to him.

"Oh…Hi, yeah, Sean, right?" he said.

"That was a great trick," I said.

"I don't know what you're talking about, man."

"Sure," I said knowingly.

I walked away, standing against the back wall of the ballroom, coat in hand. I just stood there waiting for someone to get me. Another girl came over to ask if I needed some assistance.

"You lead," I said, assuming that she would take me to Heaven.

She sat me down with another volunteer. They handed me a form to fill out for the advanced course. I just wrote "Hi" on it in big letters.

I was now sitting across from another woman who, *supposedly*, was there to persuade me to enroll for the advanced course. However, once she saw how I'd filled out the form, she said to me, "Maybe Terry can help you out."

The moment Terry sat down, I had the impression that I'd seen him somewhere before.

"You look like a game show host," I said to him.

"I do?" he replied.

"Yeah…you know, all my life I thought I would make a good game show host. What a phony way to live your life, eh?"

"Are you saying I'm a phony?"

"We're all phonies," I said.

Changing subjects, I confessed to him, "Do you know what I'm really afraid of? This part about going through the Valley of Death."

"You just went through it," he said.

"I did?" I replied in anticipation.

Heaven was close at hand. I looked to the right. For the seminar, the ballroom we were in had been divided in two. We were sitting directly across from a closed door in the room's partition.

I leaped from my chair, pushed open the door, and stepped into a magnificent site. The other half of the ballroom was completely empty, with the exception of a row of brass chairs with crimson cushions near the far wall. They looked as if they had all been especially arranged for my arrival. I admired the middle-eastern patterned carpet beneath my feet. Above, more luminescent chandeliers lit up the room.

There I was, completely alone, unsure if I would ever see another human again – and I loved it!

"Yeaaaaaaaaaaaaaaaaaaaahhhhhhhh!" I howled, as I ran around the room.

"I'm dead!"

"But what to do now?" I thought. "How do I leave this illusion of three-dimensional reality and recognize my true state of being?"

All weekend, I'd acted entirely on intuition. I just did whatever popped into my head, hoping that an inspirational key would arise, providing direction. Memories of books on attaining Nirvana passed my mind. I didn't know what I was supposed to do, but I knew it would involve *letting go of everything.*

I took off my shirt.

An Arabic guy taking the course opened the door.

"Hey, come on in, man!" I said. I thought he was coming to Heaven too.

"No, it's all right," he said. "You just do your thing, have a good time."

I thought he was blessing me for my journey.

I searched the room for a specific location to do whatever it was I was supposed to do. I also had to go to the bathroom.

"Just let go," I thought.

The first drop of urine hit the dime size center of a lotus flower in the carpet design – yet another indication that I was on the right track. My pee didn't smell bad to me anymore. It was beautiful. It smelled like it was supposed to smell – like pee.

I lay down in the small puddle I'd made, face first.

"Maybe I could push myself through the floor?" I thought. That didn't work.

Rolling over onto my back, I urinated again – this time in my Levi's.

It was all a test, wasn't it? A test to see if I was truly prepared to give up everything and surrender myself to the complete unknown.

Trembling from head to toe with energy, I thought that, perhaps, I was going to ascend piece-by-piece. As I turned my attention to my left leg, it started to shake vigorously. My mind wandering, I recalled friends who had played an essential role in my earthly existence.

"Owen!" I shouted, "Get in here!" My dive buddy never arrived. I remembered what he said to me onboard the ship, after my accident.

"So Sean, you're leaving Vancouver in three weeks to begin a new life, and you just about *lost your life* at ninety feet below sea level. Do you feel any different?"

"No, not really," I said.

"No huh?" He looked at me as if he knew something that I didn't.

Lying face-up on the carpet, I realized that Owen knew I was dead and that he was, in reality, a caretaker for me so that I could continue on my journey through Purgatory.

My leg stopped shaking and became completely relaxed. Then the other leg began to shake. I contemplated how I'd wanted to have children before I died.

"Time is an illusion," I thought.

"Lyndon!" I shouted. Lyndon was a tall, good looking, nineteen year-old guy I'd met at The Forum. We had sort of hit it off. After the third day of the seminar, I bumped into him in the cloakroom, at which point he said to me, "I love you, man!" and gave me a hug.

"Why?' I asked.

"Because you're just such a cool guy to talk to!"

It crossed my mind that perhaps I got to meet him before I died because he was my son in another life.

Then a funny thing happened.

A few seconds after calling Lyndon's name, I heard saxophone music. Lyndon was a saxophone player! He had come to The Forum to help himself learn to do other things besides practice his saxophone. As strange as it may sound, playing the sax had become a bit of an addiction for him. He was a sax addict.

Was the music I heard coming from my mind or from the "real" world? I had no idea. I was dead. Anything was possible.

My right leg relaxed along with the left leg now, as if both had died.

The energy then went to my penis.

"Take it!" I shouted.

I thought of all of the selfish things I'd done, and the negative relationships I'd developed because of my sex drive.

"Take it!" I repeated. I was happy to get rid of what I then saw as an overpowering third brain. My penis trembled, then released into lifeless relaxation.

Energy then seeped into my belly. Warm memories of friends and family surfaced as other areas shook and then released. I was ascending to Heaven one piece at a time.

I spread my arms out like Jesus on the cross.

My ribs shook violently.

"Take it! Take it! Take it!"

At the end of every shaking session, I heard a bell ring – the same high tone that signified the most sacred stages of the Catholic mass. I was on my way.

After every major body part had shaken and released, the energy finally arrived at my eyes. I thought I may be blind once this part had completed itself. For the last time, I stared into one of the chandeliers…and released. To my surprise, when I opened my eyes I could still see.

I was now completely relaxed. The energy that had overwhelmed me for four days was gone. In the ceiling, one light which I'd been staring at turned pink.

"Was it a sign of God's love?" I asked myself.

"I think so."

I heard the sacred tone of the bell one last time. Whatever I was going through was over.

Examining my hands, I thought, "You know, for being dead, this looks *really real.*"

Then in came the first security guard.

HELL

A rather intimidating black security guard entered the ballroom. I looked over at him as I lay on the carpet, shirtless, in urine soaked blue jeans. I thought that maybe he was coming to take me to the next level. He asked me what I was doing there. I was vague. He left.

Minutes later, three security guards came in, all of them black. I found this quite amusing.

"Man, there are a lot of black angels," I thought. "No wonder I've always preferred hanging out with those guys."

Two of them meant nothing to me, but the third, I thought I'd met somewhere before. My intuition was razor sharp at this point, as I could see that this third security guard was a very nice person.

"You look familiar," I said.

"Well, I've got a familiar face," he replied with a sideways smile. I wasn't sure what that meant.

After the four of us stood there for a while, the first guard said, "Come on, let's go."

"You lead," I said. Wherever we were headed, I was ready to go.

When we got to the main doors of the ballroom, the nice guard had a request.

"Here man, put your shirt on," he said.

I refused.

He gave it to me and I let it drop to the floor.

"No."

If I was going to Heaven, I was not going to hide my state in shame. I wanted to go "shirt-off." To me it was a test, a test to see if, being dead, I would still conform to the restrictions of our fear-driven society. This caused quite a dilemma. The guards left to get some of the members of The Forum staff.

The first guy to approach me was a volunteer. We'll call him Bart. He was responsible for announcing break-times over the weekend. I didn't like him when I first saw him. I didn't like him now.

He stood in front of me, looking straight into my eyes. His eyes were like ice. I knew more than ever that Bart was not to be trusted.

"What's going on, Sean?" he asked in a threatening tone. He was obviously more concerned with taking care of an unruly course member than helping me.

"What's going on?" he kept asking.

I just laughed and walked away. I despised everything he stood for – another phony controller. He was also a test, there to scare me into submission.

Thatcher came next. Unlike Bart, she was not there to hurt me, but her calm disposition couldn't hide the fact that she was scared to death.

"Sean, if you don't start to behave, something very bad is going to happen to you. Do you understand me?" she said.

I was immediately frightened. I felt the power of her words penetrate my heart. I turned and walked away from her. I then remembered what Thatcher had taught us during the seminar. Don't suppress your fear. Acknowledge it, stay with it. I did, and the fear subsided. I returned to face her. I was no longer afraid. I had overcome my fear of something bad happening to me. I had faith that everything would be okay, that something bad would not happen to me. This was another test. I was unwavering. I was brave.

"You know what you are doing," she said.

"I do?" I replied.

I was excited by this. If she thought I knew what I was doing, maybe I was on the right path. I still wasn't sure. I was just looking for clues.

She insisted that I put my shirt back on. Instead, I removed my shoes, socks, and pants. I was now in the Windsor Hotel Ballroom wearing nothing but my underwear.

Thatcher didn't say anything. She went out and grabbed a chair from the hall. I didn't realize it at the time, but a whole slew of people were on the other side of that door, trying to figure out what to do with me.

When she sat down, I sat at her feet, cross-legged.

"Were you my first grade teacher?" I asked.

"No, I wasn't," she replied, looking as if she was just trying to hold it together, Forum-style. They seemed to cultivate a type of personality that makes you act like some sort of detached robot.

I felt powerful, sitting there in my underwear. I'd tossed my glasses aside earlier, so I had a hard time seeing. But other than that, I was quite relaxed, waiting for the next test.

Just passing the time, I started talking into my shoe.

"Hello...hello...."

"You know," I said to Thatcher, "I always wondered why on Get Smart (the old TV show) they had the shoe-phone on the sole of the shoe where it would get crushed."

She nodded.

Minutes later, Thatcher exited and my dad was brought in with the head of Landmark Education, Steve Shannon. When I saw Dad, I thought he was an angel and that, perhaps, his job had to do with my spiritual growth. But, as it turns out, he was just there as another test.

"Sean, think of your mother," he said.

Once again, fear struck me in the heart. They were trying to scare me by getting me to think of how I was hurting my mother. I turned away, remaining present to how frightened that made me feel. The fear soon passed. I returned to stand before my father, bowing in reverence.

Dad then tried to convince me to come with them in some other way. What was I to say? I thought it was all a test to get into Heaven, and if I told them that, they would deny it anyway. Everyone in the ballroom had been sent there to test me, to see if I was susceptible to their threats and verbal manipulation. As they were finding out, I wasn't.

In retrospect, my actions were completely sane and quite brave when you consider the situation that I thought

I was in. It's just that I'd made an error in assessing the reality in which I was interacting…or had I?

Steve Shannon was the last Forum person to test me. He informed me that if I didn't behave, the police would be called. Again, fear struck my heart. I sat with it, then let it pass. I presented my wrists to him, letting him know that I would rather be arrested than succumb to manipulation.

I then walked over to the wooden door on the other side of the room.

"Could this be my portal to Heaven?" I asked myself. I knocked on the door a few times, then Steve came over.

"You remind me of St. Peter at the Gate," I told him.

"What are you doing?" he asked.

"Me?" I punched the doorframe like a boxer. "I'm in the fight of my life!"

And I was. I knew that nothing would ever be the same again.

Then the police arrived. They were pretty big cops. I think there were two of them.

So there we were – the two police officers, my dad, Steve Shannon and me in my underwear. I walked over to the opposite wall where there was a small light switch box. I opened it and was immediately startled. Letting go of the door, the box slammed shut.

It was quite clear to me at that point. Everyone, everything in the room was somehow a product of my mental abilities. I had created the entire scenario in my mind. In fact, my entire life had somehow been my mind's creation. I'd just been too dull to see it for what it actually was.

All I had to do to end this increasingly difficult dream of mine was to extinguish myself by turning out the ballroom lights. Basically, I thought the light switches would turn me "out" as well and that I would lose my physical existence – mutating into some unfathomable spirit form.

"You have two options," one officer informed me. "We can take you to Psychiatric Emergency or we can take you to jail."

I thought about it for a second. I was feeling pretty dramatic by this point – I mean, what the hell?

"You know, all my life I thought I would make a great game-show host, and now I get to be one," I said.

"What's my first option?" I asked him again.

"Psychiatric emergency," he repeated.

I held up my index finger.

"What's my second option?"

"Jail."

Holding up my middle finger, I now had two fingers in the air.

"I'm choosing the third option."

"What's that?" said the cop.

"It's right in front of you. I choose peace." My two extended fingers made the peace sign.

I solemnly went over to the light switch box to turn out my life.

You may think that I was just kidding myself, but in my state of mind that gesture was the equivalent of committing suicide. However, as opposed to being a cowardly act, running from life, this was a sacred ritual intended to set me free, so that I could move on to the next level. I was choosing the spirit world over the material one. This was the test that God had put in front of me.

As I went to turn out the lights (and my life), the cops approached me from behind.

"Sean, we've got nothing against you, but you've got to come with us."

They grabbed one arm each. I resisted their pull as hard as I could. My whole body was shaking. I thought that maybe I could hold them off for a while. But, once I realized I had nowhere to go, I gave in.

"Okay, okay," I said.

They pulled my arms behind my back and pushed me to the floor. My left shoulder hit the carpet pretty hard, leaving a nasty burn the size of a silver dollar. I still have the scar.

As I lay with my face squished up against the carpet, they handcuffed me behind my back.

"Thanks guys," I said to them. "I know you're just doing your job." I was pretty polite with them. I didn't want them to think I was a jerk.

Lying there, I caught a glance of the one guy's gun sitting in its holster.

"There was a day when you could have pulled that thing out, stuck it in my face, and I wouldn't have blinked," I said to him – recalling how I'd thought I was fearless. I still thought they might shoot, and I was prepared to accept that fate.

I was surprised to see the stretcher they wheeled in for me. They were very prepared, covering me with an orange sheet.

I didn't know where we were going, although they said I was being taken to the hospital. I found it all very funny. I mean, what a wild-ass ride this was, going from Earth to Heaven after you died! This big test – people trying to scare the crap out of you with threats that you will go to jail, hurt your mother, that you will die. And I passed it all.

They wheeled me out into the hotel lobby. I saw Bart, that first Forum volunteer who tried to manipulate me. I looked at him and smiled. "Goodbye," I said. There were a lot of people out in the hall, watching me pass by.

My dad was one of them. He says that to this day he will never forget seeing me being taken down and hand-cuffed by those cops.

In retrospect, I find it to be a coincidence of staggering proportions that I initially signed up for The Landmark Forum in Vancouver because I felt "handcuffed" in my career path, and here I was, *actually handcuffed* by two police officers.

But I didn't mind. I thought it was all part of the test, every step taking me closer to God. Underneath all of the chaos swirling around me, I still had a tremendous feeling of divine bliss. Plus, I still thought I was dead. Being wheeled into the hotel elevator I thought it might take us all "up" to Heaven.

Once in the ambulance, the officers remained friendly, asking if I wanted to roll onto my side, to take the pressure off of my handcuffs. I declined. I liked the handcuffs, the way they dug into my wrists as I lay on top of them. It just felt like it was supposed to be that way.

It was only in those handcuffs that I felt free. Once society puts handcuffs on you, you are free in a way that you're not in normal life. Free to speak exactly what's on your mind. Free to scream. Free to cry. Free to laugh your ass off without having to worry about offending anybody. Free not to behave like a civilized human being, which none of us actually are, but all of us pretend to be.

We're all raging storms of emotions and insecurities; wild, exotic jungles, trying to fit ourselves into cookie-cutter "lifestyles" dictated to us through the myths of our culture. I should know, I worked in advertising at the time. Even the rebels have to behave like "rebels" – the skate-punk, the techno geek, the teacher, the adman, the priest, the salesperson, the doctor. Where are the humans?

I was stunned to see that I was actually being wheeled into what appeared to be a hospital. Pushing my stretcher through the automatic sliding doors, the staff asked me to be quiet, so as not to disturb the other patients. But I didn't feel like being quiet. I kept yelling "Hi!" to anybody who walked by. I was still blissfully happy, completely oblivious to my situation. It wasn't until afterwards that I realized how seriously everyone had taken all of this. As for me, for the first time in my life, I felt free.

My time there was a little surreal. First, they put me in a hospital bed, face-down, with both arms and legs locked to the bed in restraints. I was cool with that.

Then in came a young, Chinese doctor, Dr. Chin. He looked like a nice enough guy, sitting in the chair across from me, notepad in hand.

"So, Mr. Blackwell, could you tell me what happened this evening?" I quietly laughed to myself. There I was in this "hospital," saner and more coherent than I'd ever been.

I knew that all I had to do was tell him that I'd had a reaction to The Forum brought on by my scuba diving accident; that I'd thought I was dead, but now I know I am alive, and that they would probably let me go. But I just couldn't bring myself to lie like that. I knew it was one way of interpreting my circumstances, but it did not represent my truth.

I asked Dr. Chin if I could sit up in the chair across from him so that we could talk, one human to another. He declined. Then I told him that I didn't want to deal with a *doctor*, I wanted to talk to a *person*. I asked if I could call him by his first name.

"You can call me Dr. Chin," he said. I looked at his name tag, "Dr. F Chin." From that point on I would call him by his first name, whether he liked it or not, "F."

Behind his black-rimmed glasses, "F" listened with a tilted head, which told me that he was judging, analyzing, but not really hearing me. I told him what I actually thought had happened – how I'd died and gone to The Forum, where I went through the Valley of Death.

I said it all in a rather sarcastic manner, knowing full-well that if he were a real psychiatrist (which I was almost certain he was not) my story would absolutely mean that I was insane. But I wasn't about to chicken-out now. I was sticking to my truth.

After "F," my dad came in as well. He quietly stood next to me, with a hand on my back the entire time. His hand being there was very reassuring. If he took it off, I would ask him to put it back on. I still thought that Dad was a spiritual entity, helping me return to "Heaven."

I thought the hospital room might be travelling in some way, or that I was in some sort of transformation process that he was there to guide me through. It was great having him there to babble to, and he was wise enough to avoid trying to bring me back to Earth with any more verbal manipulation.

Imagery would float through my mind almost as vivid as a hallucination. I was talking out what was in my head as fast as it would come.

Most of the imagery carried me back into my childhood, then into creation itself. At one point I was flooded with a scene from the movie, *2001: A Space Odyssey*, where a small band of apes jump around a mystical, black monolith. The experience was so strong, I felt as if I were a monkey as well. I started making ape noises on the hospital bed, "Ooo, ooo, ooo!"

Some of the imagery made me think that I was still in the process of dying: scenes from TV shows which I loved as a child, like *Sha Na Na*; visions of the cosmos related to the Big Bang; there were even a few songs as part of the evening's entertainment.

I sang Amazing Grace to myself,

"I once was lost, but now I'm found, was blind, but now I see."

"Dad, are you an angel?" I asked him.

"No," he said.

"Why not?"

"I haven't earned my wings." he said.

In the world I was in, that made perfect sense. Dad was down here assisting me in order to earn his wings.

Later, my mother arrived, followed by my brother and his wife. I was thrilled, as I thought I would never see any of them again. I asked if my roommates from Vancouver were coming as well, hoping that, perhaps, all of my friends and relatives would be able to visit me, regardless of their supposed location.

Questions like these clearly left "F" and the family with the impression that I had lost my mind entirely. But I never actually felt insane. As far as I could tell, I was operating in a completely new reality in which I didn't quite understand the rules. I asked apparently strange questions because I thought anything might be possible in this new world, where things work more like they do in a dream than they did in my old "real" life. However, just as in dreams, you don't always get what you want. In fact, you often get what you fear.

I began to realize that perhaps my take on reality may have been a little off when the doctor had some security guards and nurses change my sheets, which had become stained with the urine from my underwear. Making a small effort to be cooperative, I politely asked the guards if they wanted me to move.

"You're not moving anywhere," was the reply of one of them. His mean-spiritedness and pleasure in exerting power over me was obvious.

"You don't think I can move?"

"Aaaaaaaaahhhhhh!!!" I yelled, shifting around in my wrist and leg restraints as much as possible. The hypocrisy of the institution I was dealing with was becoming more apparent. They had no real interest in trying to understand what I was going through. They were much more concerned with controlling me than helping me. Mind you, by this point, I wasn't exactly a joy to work with either. I simply wouldn't be quiet, which is what they wanted more than anything.

I asked "F" if he was going to tell anybody about my night in the hospital.

"No, it's confidential," he replied.

"Not even your wife?" I asked.

"No," he said.

"You mean to tell me that you are never in your entire life going to tell anyone about what happened to me tonight because it's confidential? Nobody?"

"That's correct," "F" replied, in an almost too professional manner.

I began to consider the possibility that I might be considered insane by others for the rest of my life. I discovered later that the doctors had told my parents the same thing. They advised my mother that I could come out of this in a few days, or that I may have this condition, whatever it was, forever.

Five years earlier, my brother had been in a fire. His entire upper body was covered with second and third degree burns. When I first saw him after he returned from the hospital, he was completely bandaged from the waist up, like a mummy. I'd never been so shaken as seeing him lying on our living room floor, bandaged up like that, wondering if he would ever look normal again. After I got out of the hospital, Mom said that me being "insane" was the single worst experience of her life – worse than seeing my brother burned.

"I know what I'm going to do with the rest of my life!" I told Mom, holding her hand.

"People will come to examine me and try to figure out why I am the way I am, and I'll tell them what they've been waiting to hear their entire lives."

"What's that?" she asked.

"That they're okay – just the way they are, *they are okay.*"

If people only knew that, deep down, they were just fine and that most of their troubles came from defending a false image of themselves – this was the key to a whole new society. I knew what I'd learned over the weekend could change the world, and that I could be a vehicle for this change.

I guess I was also starting to consider the possibility that I might not be dead after all, and that being labeled insane by society was something that could actually happen to me. But I felt ready for the challenge. The cuffs on my wrists and ankles made me feel strong. Biblical images of Samson shattering the pillars to which he was chained flashed through my mind.

Eventually, the doctors and nurses got tired of my shtick. They took everyone out of the room, slamming shut the glass sliding door which separated them from me.

"Wait, I want to talk!" I yelled.

Everyone ignored me. I started to think, as a small child would, that because they didn't respond, they really couldn't hear me.

"Are you deaf?!"

"Are you deaf?!"

"Are you deaf?!" I shouted over and over.

Finally "F", a few nurses and a couple of security guards came back in.

"Did you hear what I said?" I sincerely asked them. I got no response.

"I asked you, 'Are you deaf?'" I was pretty damn belligerent by this point. But under the circumstances, being handcuffed to a bed and cut off from human contact, who wouldn't be? They remained strangely silent. That's when I noticed the nurse at the end of the bed holding up a large syringe.

"Get that needle away from me…I do not want that needle…I do not want that needle," I calmly pleaded.

Despite being frightened, I think I acted quite composed. I didn't know what was in that thing. I would have preferred a gun to my head. At least then I would know what was going to happen.

"Why don't we take the needle away?" suggested one of the guards.

"Terrence! Tell them! Tell them! They can't hear me!" I said, reading his name tag.

The others ignored both him and me.

I turned to "F."

"Look, if I calm down, will you take the needle away?"

"Yes," he replied.

"Okay, just give me a minute."

"Okay," he said.

I focused intensely on the nervous energy that was trembling through my body all night, trying to direct it toward my navel. I then began to breathe deeply in an effort to get myself to relax. "F" lost patience. He nodded to the security staff to force me down.

"Wait one more minute!" I asked him. "F" agreed and I was able to calm myself down. I lay with my body entirely pressed against the mattress. I also shut up.

"F" then gave the order for them to inject me.

"How am I supposed to believe anything you say when you lie to me like that!!?" I shouted at him.

I snapped around to the nurse with the needle, "How would you like it if I stuck a dick up your ass, because that's what you're doing to me!!!"

I was furious. Their betrayal made me sick.

Knowing they were going to inject me whether I liked it or not, I chose to lie still and let them give it to me so that I could reduce the risk of physical injury to my thigh upon injection.

This was rape.

"Fine, I'll take your needle if that will make *you feel better*," I said, sarcastically. "But it isn't gonna do anything!"

And they stuck it in.

With the drama of the injection over with, they pretty much left me alone for the rest of the night. It felt like I spent hours trying to get out of my restraints. Not that I minded them so much, but I was wide awake and had nothing else to do. I even asked permission from the security guard.

"Do you mind if I try and get out of my restraints?" I politely asked him.

"Go ahead, but you're wasting your time".

"All I have is time," I said. I guess it never dawned on him that I might be bored, being left alone in a dark room with nothing but a bed to play with.

At one point during the night I was handed a form which stated that the hospital had the legal right to keep me under supervision for three days. The page had a series of statements regarding my condition, which I found absolutely laughable. The worst was that, "I was a danger to myself and others." What harm had I done to anyone? I was only trying to get to Heaven.

At the bottom of the page was one line that I never thought I would come across. It stated that I had the right to a lawyer.

"I want a lawyer! I want a lawyer!" I yelled incessantly. I genuinely did want one. I wanted someone to represent me – a civilized human on my side to battle these idiots for my freedom.

"F" came back in the room.

"I want a lawyer," I said to him.

"It's 4 a.m. Can't you wait until the morning?"

"This form says I have the right to a lawyer, I want a lawyer."

The lawyer never came. I later discovered that "F" had consulted with my parents, and that they had waived off the lawyer. I'm still unsure as to what my rights were in that situation. I was thirty years old and yet my parents had the right to waive my right to legal representation? I crumpled up the document and threw it in the corner.

"F" wasn't all bad, however. Minutes after injecting me, he returned to ask my mom if I would like to be turned over, so that I would be more comfortable. By that point, I guess talking to me directly was out of the question.

I told him that I was fine.

I can't remember when I finally dozed off, but I do know why I was able to, and it had little to do with the drugs they gave me. At one point during the night my brother came to speak with me, alone.

Glen worked as a social worker at a place that troubled kids go to when they become uncontrollable at their group-homes. They are, most often, mentally ill and/or abused. To put people in restraints is a part of his job. He sees kids in my situation every day – but it was another thing to see his older, university educated brother.

Perhaps it was because he deals with this sort of thing regularly, or maybe it's just that he's a little crazy himself, but he was the first person all night who talked to me like I was still me. Nobody else had shown that kind of courage – to understand that this person locked to a hospital bed was, for the most part, a normal human being and should be treated like one.

"Sean, maybe someday you'll be able to tell me what you're going through, and maybe one day we'll sit down and talk about it. But right now, with all of your yelling, you're scaring a lot of sick people in this emergency room. So why don't you just lie down and get some sleep." It was the most honest thing anyone had said to me all night.

As nothing "otherworldly" had happened and I had seen my whole family again, I considered the possibility that I may not be dead. But moreover, by this point I realized that, if I had my choice, I wasn't ready to die, especially with what had happened to me. There was just so much more to do while I was here on Earth.

"If I go to sleep, will I wake up?" I asked Glen, still not certain of anything.

"Yeah, you'll wake up," he reassured me.

After that, I felt like everything was going to be all right and, most likely, my reality wasn't going to change much. Maybe I was dead, but if that were the case, death was going to be very similar to what life was like, at least in appearance. I knew that this new existence (either dead or alive) would be a whole lot better than the last one.

While I was asleep, the nurses wheeled me to a room in the main part of the hospital. According to my parents, I slept for about twenty-four hours straight. I remember waking up, mid-sleep, and my family was there in the room with me.

"Well, I'm either dead, or I just went off my stick!" I told them, completely bewildered by my newfound circumstances.

"He's going to be okay!" Mom said, with a laugh. It was a huge relief for her to hear me consider the possibility that I might still be alive.

A nurse then came in and persuaded me to take two pills of unknown origin. She said that they would help me sleep. I immediately liked this particular nurse. An older Caribbean woman, she sounded more like she was trying to get me to eat my vegetables. Concerned that they would mess with my mind, I didn't want to take them. But by then, I had softened somewhat, so I agreed.

"All right, I'll take them," I told her and my family. "But I'm not going to sleep now because of these pills. I'm going to sleep because I want to go to sleep." And that's just what I did.

The following day, I phoned Carmen to tell her what had happened.

"Where are you?" she asked.

"I'm in Wellesley Psychiatric."

She laughed her head off.

"My whole family takes The Forum and you wind up in the hospital!" She sort of meant it as a compliment.

I think it was later that afternoon that I had my great reckoning – the first official visit with the staff psychiatrist. All I knew was that I wanted to get out of there. Thoughts of Johnny Depp in the movie *Don Juan de Marco* passed through my mind. I gave that sort of performance.

"I had a scuba diving accident about a month ago where I could have died instantly," I told her. "I hadn't dealt with my feelings regarding that near fatality. When I went to The Forum, it led me to address that issue. That, combined with the mental stress of the course, put me in a state of mind where I believed that I was dead. But now I know I'm still alive and that I was going through some sort of post-traumatic stress disorder."

I thought that would impress her. It was all bullshit.

I still wasn't sure if I had died or not. I could have told them that story about post-traumatic stress disorder the night I went in there. I could have put my clothes on at any time. I could have stopped myself from pissing on the floor. But I chose not to. I chose to act out the inner drama of what was *really going on inside of me,* and that made all the difference.

As Mom could accurately perceive that the doctors weren't doing anything helpful with me, she asked that I be released into her custody during the day. Mom didn't trust the psychiatrists any more than I did. When asked if she wanted to take some medication home for me, she wisely declined, knowing how much the idea of being on meds would upset me. I spent the next two days with Mom at home, mostly watching TV, then returning to the hospital at night to sleep.

Four days after being admitted, I walked out of Wellesley Psychiatric Hospital for the last time. Heading for the exit, I was surprised to see Dr. "F" in the hallway. Seeing him there was no coincidence. Immediately, the moment struck me as an opportunity to make peace with this man.

"Hey!" I called over. "Listen, I just wanted to apologize for the other night, I know I was hard on you."

"F" looked at me as if he were seeing a ghost. He was completely shocked that I was the same person he had injected just a few nights earlier.

"No problem!" he enthusiastically replied. "We were just trying to help."

For the first time, I could see who my doctor actually was. The night I was admitted, the person who sat across from me was a cold, analytical man who thought he knew everything. The person in front of me now was so young, wide-eyed and inexperienced, perhaps only twenty-five or twenty-six.

His words would stay with me, "…just trying to help." Everybody is "just trying to help." They have no idea of the damage they are doing.

Nevertheless, by apologizing to him I lifted his burden and, in a way, I guess I lifted my own.

I saw very few people during my first few weeks back home. I preferred to stay inside, watch TV, or maybe sit in silence. I felt as if I'd been stripped down to my core and, while at peace with myself, I was also extremely sensitive.

It was funny to see how friends and family reacted. Some were cautious with their words, looking at me in a distant, "Is he crazy?" sort of way. Others reveled in my wild experience. When I told Wendy that I'd taken my clothes off and pissed on the carpet of the main ballroom at the Windsor Hotel, she just laughed and said, "Sean, if only that happened to everybody!"

Surprisingly, the person who was to give me the most help and guidance during this adjustment period was someone I hardly knew. Sheena was a close friend of Carmen's family and had taken The Forum back when it was called "EST Training" in the '70s. I'd talked to her at a few get-togethers before I moved to Vancouver. About ten years older than myself, she struck me as one of the most interesting, spiritual women I'd ever met. Aside from that, she also had a master's degree in psychology and was a practicing past-life therapist.

Hearing the details of my story from Carmen, Sheena asked to see me as soon as possible.

About a week after I got out of the hospital, Sheena paid me a visit. My mother sat with us in our living room as I told Sheena everything. Near the end of our conversation she asked me what I thought I had gotten out of this experience. I told her how I felt that I'd confronted all of my deepest fears – of death, of rape, of losing my parents, of being put in jail, of being naked in public, everything.

"Sean, you got it!!!" she shouted, leaping off the couch.

"I got it?"

"Yes, YOU-GOT-IT!"

"You don't need any more courses. You are in this world, but you are not of it."

Part 2

The Struggle for Integrity

Hold Your Horses

May, 1996

"Hold your horses!" they cried,
As they see the fire in my eyes,
The power of my step.

"Hold your horses!" they shriek,
As I grow from infant into Brady Bunch clothing
and matching lunch box.

"Hold your horses!"
"Hold your horses!"
"Hold your horses!"

"Okay!" I said.
I will hold my horses if that is what it takes to be loved,
If that is what will make you happy.
"I will hold my horses and do as you say."

But why?

Are my horses evil or stupid?
Are they pointless?
Are they wrong?
They must be.

For why would I want to hold my horses unless they
were horses not worth sharing?
Horses which should not run free?
Horses not worthy of love?

How could I have known the fear behind their masks,
as they witnessed the power beneath my saddle.

Nostrils flaring with anticipation,
Jaws tugging at the bit.
Limbs coiled, eyes eager, focused and ready.

Each horse, bigger, faster and more beautiful
than the last.
Effortlessly pulling behind them trains of lightning,
trains of genius;
Trains of love and beauty, all barreling dangerously
toward them at Godspeed,
Never fast enough for me.

But I succumbed.
For love, I pulled hard on my reins,
Watching my once fierce stallions soften, weaken,
and slow.

The milk wagons which replaced the trains were heavier
than the mass of the Universe.
And for what?
Warm, spoiled milk?
A pat on the head?
A paycheck?

My horses were dying one by one.
Their loads got smaller and heavier.
My paycheck to nothing.

Impotence replaces Passion,
Resignation replaces Curiosity,
Mediocrity replaces Genius,
Apathy replaces Love.

But my horses are held,
And my horses die with me.

Death, Fear of Death, Dreaded Death.
Oh God! Not Death!
"We must survive, even if it kills us!" is their mantra.

But I did not care when Death came for me.
Take me Sweet Death,
Take my horses too,
And let us have our trains,
Let us have our power,
Let us run, run again, roughshod over terrain unknown!

Through the eyes and hearts of a billion souls,
Lost and Confused,
Afraid to Live, Afraid to Die.

Take me sweet death and give me back my horses.
Give me back my trains and let me run the Earth with
creativity and love and lightning.

Lightning to empower others with what is within them
that they do not know.
Lightning to destroy that which keeps them from
knowing and loving themselves.
Lightning that heats the air around it,
that brings life.

Take me Sweet Death, and send me back to this
Planet of God.
But send me as I am, Anew!
For I am no longer a child,
and I will not hold my horses.

SENSITIVITY

From the very beginning of my experience, there was never any doubt in my mind that I was going through a profound spiritual transformation. The notion that I could possibly have a mental illness struck me as positively absurd. When the family gently suggested that I, perhaps, see a psychologist, my response was, "Why would I talk to someone who has no idea of what just happened to me?"

It was a rhetorical question.

But how to take this new "me" and insert him back into daily life was another matter.

All my life I'd felt uneasy inside, unable to sit still. Like many "normal" people, I went to nightclubs and bars to blow off steam and burn energy. But now I felt very calm at the center of myself, much more at ease and gentle. However, I was also much more emotional because I had become far more sensitive.

Fargo was the first movie I went to see, shortly after my hospitalization. The violence and gore of this supposed comedy hit me so hard I almost needed to leave the theater.

I had similar feelings visiting a local rave with some friends of mine. The thumping bass vibrating out of the speakers seemed to be attacking my body. I could not leave soon enough.

Fortunately, for my first six months out of the hospital I didn't need to work too much. David Stone was only interested in "testing me out" on a few projects, so I was usually at WeCU only one or two days a week. This was exactly what I needed, as it took the family pressure off me to find full-time work. Instead, I could simply stay home and integrate my experience.

Following Sheena's recommendations, I read a few books that she had found to be most enlightening, starting with *Autobiography of a Yogi*, the story of Paramahansa Yogananda.[1] As time passed, I invested in a vast array of spiritual materials, exploring this previously untapped dimension of my existence as never before. I also began meditation classes with Guru Satyam, a Kriya Yoga instructor from India.

Other aspects of my life changed as well. I would often have psychic experiences, to the point where I started to see life as simply a physical dream.

One morning, I was alone in our kitchen having my typical breakfast of cereal and orange juice. Staring out our backyard window, I was struck with an intuition to open the front door, at the opposite end of the house. Standing there was a cute Chinese girl, just about to knock.

"Wow!" she exclaimed. "ESP or what!"

It's important to know that in our quiet Canadian suburb, we may not have anyone knock on our door in an entire week. As it turns out, the girl was originally from

Vancouver and had just started working for a charitable organization. She was in the neighborhood asking for donations. We had a nice conversation.

Another day I was relaxing at home, talking on the phone with Trevor, a close friend of mine from university. I hadn't seen him since my hospitalization. After a long chat about my experience, he asked me what I wanted to do that day. Closing my eyes, I could see long brown reeds on a mud flat. I told him about this vision I was having, and that I wanted to walk through the reeds. Of course, this was fantasy to me, as I had no idea if the field I was seeing even existed.

I then drove out to Trevor's new home in Mississauga, about an hour away, not sure what the day would bring us. Being my first visit there, he took me on a tour of his neighborhood. Within a mile of his home was the same field of reeds I'd seen in my vision, with a twisting creek surrounding it on three sides, explaining why the ground was so muddy.

Being part of a public park, there were many people there on this Sunday afternoon. Meandering across the mud flat of reeds, with the crisp, blue sky above us, we spent the rest of the day pondering my recent experiences and new-found insights.

While it was hardly something that I looked forward to, the death of my grandmother would have strong psychic aspects as well. My mother's mother, Margaret, was the grandparent who I felt closest to. Sure, she bitched a lot, smoked too much and her cooking was usually scary, but I always looked to her as a true guardian. Whenever we were sick or in trouble, I knew she would be praying for us every night. And while she had an ornery exterior, all I had to say to her was, "I love you," and she would get all choked up.

The night before she died, I thought I was dying in my sleep. The dream was so vivid that mucus started blocking my nasal passages and I had to wake myself up to continue breathing. Once again, I thought it was me who was bound for Heaven. That morning, we got a call from the hospital. Mother Margaret had less than twelve hours left.

Gathered by her bedside, some of the family found my behavior a little odd. I was still in such a positive frame of mind that it appeared to others that I may have been clueless as to what was actually happening. My episode had occurred less than two months earlier.

To be honest, I was happy for her. She had been living with a lot of pain for quite a while. I wasn't exactly sure what was wrong with her, but she apparently had a number of complications related to the cancer surgery she'd had a few months earlier.

Moments after she passed away in her hospital bed, I sat alone, off to the side, in sacred silence. I had the desire to simply be quiet, to see if she would communicate anything to me.

"Huh? That's strange." I thought to myself.

Closing my eyes, I had a vision of Grandma as she was at about forty years of age. The trouble was, I didn't know her at that time. I wasn't born until she was over fifty.

"Why am I imagining Grandma like this?"

As she was much younger and smiling, I took it as a message that she was fine.

At home, for the first time after the funeral, my parents and I were sitting in the living room together.

"I know I should be sad," my mother said, "but I just see her with this big smile on her face!"

"What was she wearing?" I asked.

"She had on a dark brown blouse with buttons in the front."

"And no sleeves," I added.

"That's right, no sleeves," she said.

"How old was she?" I asked.

"About forty years old."

We had both seen her in the exact same way. Grandma resembled a picture she had on her wall, standing with her four kids, during a happier, maybe the happiest, time of her life.

Years later, while reading *The Tibetan Book of Living and Dying*, I came across a passage which said that, in the Tibetan Buddhist belief system, if we have a good death the body in which we find ourselves in the afterlife is one from when we were at the peak of our vitality, not the elderly body we leave behind.[2] Apparently, Grandma was doing just fine.

Other aspects of my dream life took on increased significance as well, but it wasn't all "peaches and cream." In the beginning, I had vivid nightmares almost every night. This bothered me quite a bit. If I "GOT-IT" as Sheena said, why so many nightmares?

I came to realize that these dreams reflected traumas or fears which still laid within me, and that I had to engage much of this on a dream level in order to let it go.

I would often dream that I was being raped. I could feel a hand press down on the back of my neck, pushing my shoulder to the ground as some unknown man had sex with me. As frightening as this was, over time I learned that I had to accept this experience if I was to get over it, and that the reason for this nightmare was to realize that I was not my physical body, that I was a spirit in the casing of a body. Was this particular nightmare related to my hospitalization? Perhaps.

Over time, I would also explore lucid dreaming, the ability to awaken inside your dream and consciously control your movements within the dream itself. Each night, after meditating for about an hour, I would pray to God to bring me a lucid dream. They started occurring regularly.

Whenever I would awaken within the dream, I would begin to fly, often through walls, simply to test out this other form of reality.

One night, I awoke in what appeared to be a sparsely decorated Tokyo apartment. In the distance I could see some people socializing in the living room. Upon realizing that I was dreaming, I leaped upwards to fly through the ceiling, only to find myself arriving in the apartment above. With each leap, I found myself in another apartment, then another. Determined to fly right out of this building, I continued. Finally, I leaped through the last ceiling and into black nothingness. There, floating in space, I witnessed what appeared to be a procession of multi-colored medieval saints, frozen-still, one after the other, in the spiral shape of a DNA double-helix. As I gasped in astonishment at this incomprehensible image, I kept repeating, as if asking for help, "I don't understand, I don't understand, I don't understand…"

I immediately found myself in the home of an old Chinese mystic. My black robe contrasted nicely with the traditional red décor of his small abode. The monk approached me with a pair of black slippers, knelt down, and slipped them on my feet.

I woke up with the distinct feeling that I had somehow graduated. I'd earned these slippers by passing through this experience. The spirits, or at least this particular monk, were proud of me.

VALIDATION

A long with exploring my dream world, I was also searching for some sort of intellectual understanding of my experience outside of the spiritual traditions. It took some time, but I eventually discovered the work of Dr. Stanislav Grof, a Czech psychiatrist now living in the United States. Dr. Grof was one of the founders of trans-personal psychology in the late 1960s.

His books were a revelation to me. I can't express what a relief it was to finally find a respected psychiatrist who could explain, in detail, what I had been through. In his book, *The Stormy Search for the Self*, Grof documents a wide range of what he refers to as "spiritual emergencies." Basically, his idea was that people undergoing profound spiritual transformations can often enter periods of what may look like insanity. In fact, even the individuals in crisis may think of themselves as insane for a period of time. However, if allowed to work through their "madness" in a supportive environment, many people may find these powerful experiences to be extremely therapeutic.

The symptoms Dr. Grof listed as part of this condition mirrored my own: a high energy level; extreme emotions; a sense of oneness; timelessness; identification with one or more gods, angels or spirits; a feeling of being tested by God; a confrontation with death; a tremendous feeling of love; often terrifying fears; delusions; etc. It was as if he had been right there with me.[3]

According to Grof, experiences like these have occurred since the beginning of time and are well known among tribal peoples. In fact, shamanic initiation is often associated with having such an experience. As a result, for tribal peoples, journeys to the "Other Side" are hardly considered a mental illness – quite the opposite, in fact.[4]

The spirit world is a place where valuable insight and knowledge is acquired by the shaman, in order to help those in the tribe lead more prosperous, harmonious lives.[5]

I would eventually purchase four of his books, all of which were extremely insightful. The following year, I attended a workshop Dr. Grof was giving in Vermont on Holotropic Breathwork. This technique allows you to access the higher, spiritual, "holotropic" mind states in which you can release repressed emotional trauma.

I still remember the passion of one of his assistants as she leaned over to me saying, "Dr. Grof will not be recognized for his work in his own lifetime." The certainty of her words inspired me.

Holotropic Breathwork proved to be a fascinating technique. The combination of powerful music with accelerated breathing took me on an inner journey quite similar to the one I had in the emergency room of the hospital, except that this time I was in total control.

Lying on a mat in a hotel ballroom (not *unlike* the one I was arrested in a year earlier), once again I was flooded with imagery and emotions. As opposed to feeling like an ape, this time it was a Bengal tiger which rose within me. While I didn't regress into my childhood, I did seem to go through a birth process where it was me who was giving birth! I was surprised and a little disturbed to see my own hips flex forward, as if I were pushing out the baby.

A great deal of muscle tension was also released, particularly in my jaw. For over ten minutes, I felt like a bystander as my teeth chattered non-stop. I was not cold at all. It was the release of emotional tension that caused the chattering. By the end of the session, which lasted three hours, I was feeling deeply relaxed.

Perhaps the best part of the technique was its gentleness. Even though I was in contact with the same sort of material I had encountered while in my "divine madness" I could easily slide back into our everyday reality at any point during the session without a problem.

Eventually, I was able to track down a transpersonal psychologist who had been trained by Dr. Grof, living a few hours from Toronto. After sending him the details of my story, we agreed to meet. Our meeting was held over lunch in downtown Toronto. I was a little apprehensive, meeting my first psychologist, but he was a real "hippie" type and his wife was very warm, so things went well.

It wouldn't take long before I started crying during our conversation, a pattern which would be repeated many times over the next decade. Much to my embarrassment, I simply couldn't speak of the experience without tears of gratitude coming to my eyes. To know from personal experience that, not only does God exist, but He/She/It exists *through you and all of mankind*, remains a gift which touches the depths of my heart.

As we got to know each other, I took a quick glance over some of the comments he had made in the margins of my text.

"Oh, what a lucky man, he was..." the doctor had written.

"What did you mean by this?" I asked him. Apparently, they were words from a 1960s folk song.

He then looked at me with the utmost sincerity, "This has never happened to me," he said.

He was envious. I couldn't believe it.

Here was a man who had been a spiritual seeker all of his life and yet, approaching sixty, he somehow felt like he had missed something by not experiencing what I had been through. Rather than pathologizing my experience, this doctor revered it.

COMPROMISE

Trying to function "normally" came slowly. I often felt out-of-sorts around people, like I was alive and they were all still dead. Typical conversations about sports, relationships and the latest movie release bored me. I had to watch what I said around family and friends.

As my poem, *Hold Your Horses*, reflects, I left the hospital with the sincere intention of helping others. I soon discovered that altruism is not always as easy as it looks. I felt a need to improve all of my relationships at once, save all my friends and make everyone happy. Over time I withdrew my missionary zeal, as I realized that it was a futile, egocentric and possibly destructive approach. My newfound "enlightenment" wasn't exactly scoring huge points with those that mattered. Eventually, I learned to mostly keep my mouth shut about it, only sharing my most personal thoughts and feelings with Sheena.

While my initial attempts at saving the world were not exactly a smashing success, being part of the "solution," not part of the "problem" became a goal which I was determined to reach. Central to this issue was what to do about my career.

Even though the project work I was occasionally doing with David Stone at WeCU was going well, working in advertising tugged at my integrity stronger than ever. More and more, I felt uncomfortable with my whore-like existence in that business.

As a result, despite being unemployed, broke and living with my parents at the age of thirty, I was actually having reservations about returning to advertising. The trouble was, what else could I do? The only other idea I had was to walk to Mexico.

One night, I was discussing this dilemma with my mother. She had a difficult time empathizing with my situation, especially because I appeared to be on the cusp of landing a job which I had coveted for my entire career.

"But I'm a prostitute!" I told her.

Retiring to my bedroom in frustration, I resumed reading *Your Psychic Potential* by M. J. Abadie. It had a tacky title, but I enjoyed reading this woman's New Age perspective, as well as her various techniques for getting "in-touch" with your subconscious, "True Self" or Soul.

As luck would have it, Ms. Abadie had a history of career struggles herself. In fact, just minutes after discussing my career frustrations with my mother, I was reading of how Ms. Abadie had lived through the same difficulties I was experiencing, at the same age, no less. Before becoming an author, she'd worked as an advertising art director! Abadie left the business because she felt that advertising was "ludicrous."[6] Struck by the synchronicity of reading her story of leaving advertising only minutes after discussing the same thing with my mother, I returned to the living room to share what had happened. As I should have known, the significance of this event would be lost on my parents.

Your Psychic Potential also held another small gem. Halfway through the book was a simple visualization exercise to help discover the nature of your True Self. The exercise was hardly innovative, as I had done similar ones in the past. It involved visualizing a trail that passed through a forest. Along this imaginary walk, you would come across a body of water, a key, a chest, and a cup. At the end of the walk, up on a hill, would be a house. Approaching the home, you were then asked to explore its contents.[7]

During the visualization, I imagined a decrepit, old Victorian house, similar to the one from the classic horror movie, *Psycho.* On the front porch sat a smiling skeleton in a rocking chair. As I entered the house, I wandered from room to room, perusing the cob-webbed covered contents. Heading upstairs to the master bedroom, I again met the skeleton, except this time he was standing beside me. Together, we opened the top drawer of a dresser where we found plane tickets which the skeleton handed me – nice guy!

After the exercise, I returned to the book to decipher the meaning behind each of the symbols I'd encountered on my walk. To my disappointment, it was written that the house revealed my most heartfelt, unconscious goals.[8]

"I want this crappy old house?" I asked myself. No, clearly this was not the case. So I decided to enter back into the visualization again. What was it that this Victorian house represented? The answer was clear. It was symbolic of my stale Canadian existence with all of its Victorian trappings and expectations. I hated that house.

So what did I want to do with it?

Burn it!

I imagined myself torching the old grey house to the ground. I took great pleasure in seeing it go up in flames.

And what was left? Behind the ashes, on the other side of the fence were rolling hills of tall, wild grasses. I hopped the fence to explore the new territory. I liked it over there. I felt free.

So there it was – on a subconscious level I knew that I wanted to destroy my life.

But I think I'll keep those plane tickets.

Adding to my quest for an alternative to my advertising career, I sought the help of more than a few psychics and one very interesting astrologer. At Sheena's suggestion, I drove two hours to meet a middle-aged, female astrologer who lived on a farm near Lake Erie. She had quite a few interesting things to say.

Examining my chart, she could see that my twin desires for a spiritual life and a successful career were paramount. She also recognized how positively stuck I had been in my career for the previous four years. It was as if there had been "no way out" for me during that time period. As I had given her little information on my background, I was impressed that she was able to pick that up.

Then came the shocker. As she drew an outline of the Holy Grail chalice on a blank sheet of paper, she told me, "Based on your passion for spirituality and your career ambitions, I think that the only profession that will satisfy your thirst, will be to become a writer."

"A writer!" I replied in disbelief.

She wasn't the first person to have mentioned this idea to me. On three occasions different women, including my brother's wife, had said the same thing. Back in Vancouver, my boss had signed my going away card, "Start writing those memoirs." Once at a party, Wendy introduced me to her friends, spontaneously blurting out, "Everyone, this is Sean and he's going to write a book one day."

Personally, becoming a writer had never crossed my mind. I always thought of writers as "other people" who were either smarter or luckier than I was. It's with a touch of irony that I am sitting here writing a book as "a writer" a decade later. Of course, I'm not quite ready to quit my day job just yet.

While having a career as a rich and famous author certainly sounded enticing, considering the circumstances, I was compelled to follow a more pragmatic path. However, in order to rectify the split between the "Spiritual Sean" and the "Survival Sean," I negotiated a deal with myself. I would return to advertising, giving it my best, but I would also follow every dream or opportunity which could help me pursue my spiritual calling. Like many people, it was my hope that I would eventually be able to find a way to survive doing some sort of spiritual work.

Being hired by David Stone in September came as no surprise, as I had envisioned starting at that time with him back in May, five months earlier. How I came to close the deal was a real turning point for me.

After working for David on-and-off for about three months, we went for a coffee together to discuss how I was doing. He quickly cut to the chase and told me that, while he liked me a lot, he simply wasn't in a position to hire someone in his tiny, three-person operation who was without significant account planning experience.

At that moment, I sat coolly, as all of the previous rejections from planning positions passed my mind. Somehow, they had all felt like some sort of conspiracy. The world was out to screw me and I didn't know why.

"Here is the point where you schlep off into the sunset with your head down and your tail between your legs. Just like the others, he's been bullshitting you all along," I could hear the "Old Sean" thinking.

But along with this tired, old voice was a stillness within me that could see a fresh perspective – a new possibility. Being able to see that instant with such clarity, I was able to steer my life away from another rejection.

I calmly leaned in toward David as if he'd just told me he didn't want another cup of coffee, "Listen, I've heard that you also do a lot of commercial testing, involving data analysis, and that you need to do all of the work yourself because nobody else in the office can analyze the data. Is that right?"

"Yeah, pretty much," he said.

I knew having to analyze the data himself was a sore spot for David, but that nobody else in the office had the ability to do it properly. Most "ad people" aren't so great with numbers.

"Well, I have an extensive background in data analysis and a degree in sociology. For your next project, why don't you give the data to me as a test to see what I can do with it?"

"Now, if you can do that…"

A few weeks later, David got a look at my data analysis and I was hired. My first year at WeCU was the happiest of my career.

Thank you, Landmark Forum!

VISION

Not only my material life, but my spiritual life was also given a huge boost in September of 1996. It was during those first few weeks with WeCU that I experienced a dream that would eventually have a huge transformational impact on my life for years to come:

September 13, 1996

I was trekking through a grassy valley when a Peruvian woman up ahead pointed to me, giving hand gestures indicating that I should quickly climb a hill on my right-hand side. Following her guidance, I ascended a small plateau, only about twenty feet higher than where I'd been walking.

Once there, I found a small group of Incas, about eight of them, dressed in their cultural apparel. Next to them stood one attractive blonde woman. Recognizing that she must have been a tourist as well, I immediately joined her.

I was startled and excited by the fact that I could see the auras of all the Incas standing before me. But at this point, nobody was saying anything because they were all standing in a row, looking at the sun. It became apparent to me that I had stumbled across a ritual of some sort.

I looked up with them and, to my amazement, I could stare directly into the Sun. But, instead of its normal yellow, the Sun appeared as if it were made of liquid silver, emanating a metallic light. Then, what the Incas had been waiting for happened. The Sun extended a wand of golden light down toward the Earth. As the wand began to swing back and forth, it dawned on me what I was witnessing.

"I know what this is," I said to the blonde girl. "That wand of light is the Sun's penis. We should be able to feel the wind shift with its sway."

I extended my arms in the air, trying to feel the wind. I had a difficult time judging whether or not it was in synchrony with the Sun's swinging penis. This whole process left me with the unmistakable notion that the *Sun is conscious* – it knew it was performing in this ritual with the Inca, and they were aware of this as well.

Right in the middle of this remarkable spectacle, the Incas descended the plateau in a matter-of-fact, humble manner. For them, this was just their regular communi-cation with the Sun and, although sacred, certainly nothing out of the ordinary. The only one who stayed behind was the blonde girl.

Once all of the Inca had left, the Sun did something else that only the girl and I witnessed. The penis turned into a minute-hand, with the rest of the Sun splitting into pieces, creating a giant clock in the sky; a clock of silver light against the sky blue background.

Apparently, the Inca didn't need to witness this mystery, for they had seen all that they needed. The minute-hand started spinning faster and faster. The girl and I marveled at this spectacle for a while, then walked off the hill together to talk about it. The Sun had apparently been sending us a personal message about time accelerating – perhaps a foreshadowing of what is to occur in the future.

I'm not sure what the dream meant, but it had enough of an impact on me that I can say, if there was ever a place that is calling me, it's Peru.

A few weeks later, I followed up with this passage:

October 5, 1996

Back on September 13th I wrote down a dream that I did not quite understand – about being part of an Inca ceremony. This, along with documentaries I've seen on Peru as well as books like *The Celestine Prophecy* (which refers to ancient Inca culture), have me very interested in this region. In fact, after a psychic asked me if I felt called to any place on Earth, I only thought of Peru.

I told this to Sheena and she just started laughing, because she had been thinking the same thing. But as I mentioned before, it was the dream itself that was so compelling.

I've watched countless documentaries on shamans and tribal peoples. Why Peru? Why the Inca and not the Aztecs, the Mayan, the Inuit? Why not the Japanese, the Hindu, the Thai? Why this calling to Peru?

And what was the meaning of the clock spinning in my dream? Why did the Inca in my dream leave after the Sun began to wave its penis in the sky, leaving the blonde girl and me to watch?

I received my answer in a classic case of the Universe showing me the door, but me having to walk through it. On Wednesday of this week I went wandering by the Omega Center, where I buy all of my spiritual books.

I guess the Peru thing was on my mind, along with more of a focus on mysticism and shamanism now, so I picked up a magazine I'd glanced at once or twice before called the *Shaman's Drum*, Summer, 1996.

On page five was a full page ad that read:

INCA SHAMANISM
with Alberto Villoldo, Ph.D.
And
THE INCA MEDICINE PEOPLE OF PERU
MEET THE LAST OF THE INCA SHAMAN
THE Q'ERO ELDERS' JOURNEY
TO NORTH AMERICA
...DETROIT NOV. 23 * NEW YORK NOV. 24 *

"In an unprecedented journey this Fall, the Inca Elders of Peru will travel to North America to share their most holy rites-of-passage. The last descendants of the Inca have remained in monastic isolation for five hundred years, high in the mist-shrouded, sacred mountains of southern Peru. According to ancient prophecy, it is the time of the great gathering and reintegration of the Peoples of the Four Directions, bringing renewed order and harmony in the universe. The Q'ero believe it is time to release their teachings to the West, in preparation of the day the Eagle of the North and the Condor of the South will fly together again. The Inca are the **"Keepers of the Time to Come,"** and the rites-of-passage to who we are becoming. The Inca elders will lead us in the rites of initiation to who we are becoming individually, and to our collective destiny.

This will be a rare opportunity to meet the Q'ero masters, the last of the Inca Shaman, on this historic journey to North America.

ALBERTO VILLOLDO, Ph.D. is a psychologist and medical anthropologist, trained for over twenty years in classical Shamanism. He is founder of the Self-Regulation Laboratory at San Francisco State University and the author of numerous books including *Island of the Sun* and *Dance of the Four Winds.*[9]

There was the explanation of my dream. The Inca left the ritual once they had received their signal from Father Sun, waving them north, up the ravine from which I had come; north to North America, to initiate my people, Western Man, into their rites-of-passage.

The "Keepers of Time" are the Inca, as symbolized by the Sun morphing into a clock, and Time is being accelerated into eternity. The reason the Inca left before the Sun turned into a clock was two-fold. First, they had received the message they needed in order to begin this most sacred of journeys. Second, the clock was a message for me. It was there to let me know that the Inca would be arriving and that I am to play a role. Much change will ensue if I engage the Inca on their quest.

About a month later I drove, alone, to attend the meeting with the Inca Elders. It was a brief ceremony held just outside of Flint, Michigan. About 200 people attended. There, the Inca introduced us to their culture and initiated us into their highest rites of passage. One of the elders looked just like the only one of the eight I had seen clearly in my dream. Interestingly, there were about eight elders on the trip. As part of the ceremony, they cleansed our luminous body, or auric field. This helped explain why I was able to see their auric fields in my dream. The entire experience matched up with my dream perfectly.

As simple as these people were, they had some interesting insights regarding American culture, "You have so much, and yet nobody is connected. Everyone is alone." They also added that, "Your minds are much more developed than ours, but your hearts are not developed at all."

They were a very observant people. I returned from the ceremony inspired, and planned on visiting these same people in Peru the following year.

Meanwhile, on the material side, my first year as an account planner was going startlingly well. Starting at $35,000 per year, David gave me a $5,000 bonus at Christmas, along with $5,000 raises after three months, eight months and fifteen months, simply because he was happy with my work and my attitude. At the end of my second year with him, WeCU was purchased by a larger agency and my salary was again increased to $65,000!

Needless to say, David and our clients were very satisfied with my work. But there was something else that really made the difference. Every so often, David would hear from somebody about how "involved" or "present" I was on their project. When I was in a meeting, I was *in the meeting*. It left people feeling that I genuinely cared about their business, which I did. This stood in stark contrast to what was said about me at my last performance appraisal in Vancouver, where I was described as being constantly distracted or not paying attention. It's surprising just how important simply being fully present to the people you are with is to them, yet this phenomenon is something which we are only beginning to understand.

Within the family, my combination of newfound material prosperity and heightened spirituality earned me the nickname, *Guru Show-Me-the-Money*. I found it a little sad that some people saw me as being somewhat hypocritical in aspiring to earn more money. I've never seen a problem with it. My issue was in how you earn it. If you can do it with integrity, so be it. As for my integrity, during those first few years, I was far from perfect, but I was doing the best I could.

With this sudden success in the material world, serious worries regarding my mental health disappeared. My parents' only concern was that I showed no sign of stopping my quest for greater spiritual understanding. They worried that a powerful spiritual experience may lead to another crisis. I could see where they were coming from, but at the same time, I'd already decided that I was taking this journey to the very end.

As part of that journey, I went to Peru to visit those same Inca shamans in November of 1997.

Arriving in Lima, setting foot on Latin American soil for the first time, I felt like I'd just stepped into the middle of a military coup. Armed soldiers guarded the airport. The streets were dirty and crowded, the air polluted. It was definitely the Third World. My trip got off to a friendly, but rough start, as I spent my first night in Lima vomiting out the local alcoholic beverages in my hotel room.

Meeting most of the tour group in the morning, we immediately flew to Cuzco, where our journey into the world of the Inca would begin. Along with Dr. Villoldo, we were accompanied by two Inca shaman, Don Umberto, (who looked familiar from my dream the year before) as well as the head elder shaman, Don Manuel. For these two men, to share their rituals and beliefs with us was the fulfillment of their life's work, so our tour was as important for them as it was for us.

I was the lone Canadian on the trip. I'd flown down with five Americans – four "New Age" women and one filthy rich son of an oilman from Oklahoma. Little did I know, the majority of the tour was from São Paulo, Brazil. In the multicultural city of Toronto, I'd only ever met one Brazilian. I literally knew nothing of the place. Fortunately, most of them spoke a little English, as I spoke no Portuguese whatsoever.

Among the Brazilians was one petite, red-haired girl that joined the tour a little later. Her name was Ligia (*Lee-jee-ah*) and she met the group upon our arrival in Cuzco. She had traveled from São Paulo to Cuzco through Bolivia.

"A woman travelling alone in Bolivia?" I thought. "Interesting." However, while Ligia looked enticing, romance was not on my agenda. I was a man on a mission.

It was in the Inca Valley that our group assembled for our first meeting. There, I had an opportunity to share my angst over my career with everyone on the tour.

"I make lies for a living!" I told them.

Revealing that I was from the world of advertising was met with a laugh. I also shared with them the story of my spiritual awakening and subsequent hospitalization.

Later, I asked the shaman, "Do you know why I am here? Why are you in my dreams?"

As they only spoke Quechua, the original native language of the Inca, translations were difficult, but I think they dodged my question at the time – too soon, I suppose.

The journey would prove to be unforgettable. Every day we traveled by bus or train to some remote Inca ruin where the shamans performed ancient rituals on us, usually cleansing our auric field.

After about four days on the tour, we arrived at Machu Picchu. Initially, I was somewhat disappointed by the high level of tourism there. In photos, all you see is this mystical, ancient city situated in an impossibly remote location. What they don't show is the hotel, restaurant and parking lot just outside the picture frame.

During the day, Machu Picchu was chock-full of tourists, and our guide spoke in super-slow motion. I never thought a place so interesting could seem so dull. More often than not, I'd catch myself looking for Ligia.

Luckily, Alberto had something special in store for us after sundown. He had contacts at Machu Picchu who permitted us to enter the city at night. This time our tour was the only group on the grounds. We were led to the Death Stone, where one of the Inca's most sacred rituals would be performed on us by Don Manual. I'll admit, I was caught completely off-guard when Alberto asked that I help him with the ritual.

Arriving at the Death Stone that night, the entire group slipped into a spontaneous, sacred silence. Looking skyward, an expansive circle of clouds had gathered around the full moon, especially for our ceremony. We could all *"feel it in the air"* that night.

In his native ceremonial dress, Don Manuel had each person in the group lie on the Death Stone. One by one, he purified our energy centers with his ancient hands, then released our spirits from our bodies, literally sending them around the entire world, then back into us.

My job was to hug each person who came off the rock, "as if they were your first born child," Alberto instructed. I was grateful for the opportunity and did not want to disappoint. I recalled lying in the hospital bed, thinking to myself, "You can love everybody. It doesn't matter who they are or what they do. Everybody can be loved."

And that's what I did. I hugged each person who came to me with all I had. The reactions from people, especially the Brazilians, were wonderful. They couldn't stop talking about it afterwards. For some of them, my hug was more important than the shamanic healing.

The day after the ritual, one of the women came to me with a gift, a Peruvian doll. She communicated to me that this doll, which held a baby, was symbolic of her being born into my arms. I still have the doll and she travels with me on all of my journeys.

I must confess that during the ceremony there was one small violation on my part. After their healing, each person came off the Death Stone usually crying or expressing some form of sadness. But when Ligia descended from her rebirth, she came to me with the biggest, warmest smile I'd ever seen. For the others, there was a hug, but for her, it was a kiss on the mouth. I could not resist.

I was the last to receive the ritual. Over eighty years of age, Don Manuel was an ancient, gnomish figure right out of National Geographic. With the stars behind him, I felt as if I were an Inca myself. This was the real deal. First, he focused on my head, then chest. When he got to my belly, for some reason, he struggled. He kept pushing on the right side of my intestines, again and again. Finally, on the left side I felt a release.

"This little guy knows what he is doing!" I thought to myself.

He stopped working on me as soon as I felt that release. Don Manuel's medicine was powerful. For the next twenty-four hours I was stuck in my hotel room with diarrhea. I was so ill that I missed our morning hike up the main mountain, to where the group could overlook Machu Picchu from above.

After our forbidden kiss (which she did not object to), Ligia and I spent more time together, but as we were in "travel mode," neither of us was taking anything too seriously. But, as the days passed, she began to have a familiar feeling to me – independent, funny, introspective, spiritual. She reminded me…of me!

Finally, about ten days into the trip, I sat down next to her on the bus.

"What is your birthday?" I asked her.

"March 27th," she replied.

I knew it.

"That's my birthday!" I told her. Refusing to believe me, she asked to see my passport. After that, the connection became stronger.

A few days later, we were having pizza together, alone, just the two of us. I asked her a second question.

"What time were you born?"

Many people don't know the time they are born, but I knew she would.

"11:30 in the morning," she replied.

I almost fell off my chair.

"Exactly as I thought."

We were born on the same day at the same time.

As our trip neared its end, the two shamans read coca leaves for the group in private readings. I was a little nervous waiting for my turn, as I had a feeling that my session would be an important one.

Entering his tent, I told Don Umberto of my dream from the year earlier, and that this dream was the reason I'd come to Peru. I asked him why I was there, and if my career in advertising was really what I should be doing.

Don Umberto informed me, quite directly, that I was in Peru because Mother Earth (Pachamama) had called me there in my dream, and that shamanism would be my work in the future, not advertising. He said that the reason I was cut out for this work was that I knew, "…in my heart what thousands of people are searching for in books and cannot find." His reading confirmed my deepest suspicions about myself. I wept in gratitude.

In fact, I'd been crying all through the trip. My tears perplexed a lot of people. It's just that the whole experience felt so sacred to me, every minute of it. I was also some-what confused. "Am I still dreaming?" I would ask myself. "What is reality?" "Why is this happening to me?"

On our last day of the tour, Don Umberto took me, Ligia and a few of the other Americans up to a sacred site in Cuzco. There, as we had done on the entire tour, we performed long detailed rituals of sincere intention. We sat for hours creating "despachos" of coca leaves, candies, special stones and other materials as gifts for Mother Earth.

At one point, I noticed some tourists (and a local dog) watching us from a distance.

"In the beginning, we were *on* the tour. Now we *are* the tour!" I told Ligia. The connections we'd formed with our two shamans as well as the deep respect we had for their spiritual practices made us feel almost as if we were Inca ourselves.

As our ceremony came to a close, Don Umberto grabbed my hands, speaking to me with a passion he had not shown until now. Everything he said was in Quechua. I didn't understand a word, but I understood everything. His message to me was simple, "Keep going. Don't stop. You are on the right track."

Afterwards, he brought together Ligia and me, blessing us as a couple. I thought that was pretty funny. We were together a lot on the tour, but, as she lived half-way around the world from Toronto, I don't think either of us saw our relationship as something long-term. It was simply a very special "vacation" romance.

We spent our last night in Peru together, sharing a small bed – my first with a woman in over two years. When the Sun rose, I had to rush off to catch the bus to the airport. The trip was over. Ligia kissed me farewell with a some-what vacant look on her face. My painfully quick exit left us both feeling out-of-sorts.

"I'll see you again," I told her. I don't think she believed me at the time, but what she didn't know was the feeling I had for her. No, I can't say that it was exactly one of true love – more like a passionate, insatiable desire to *talk* to this woman. Despite the language barrier, we never, ever, ran out of conversation. When we were together, life was light, fun, interesting and meaningful. Every moment.

"Because of all the rituals we've been doing, our energy is very strong and pure now." At least that's what Alberto told us before we left. I didn't pay much attention at the time, however, once I arrived at Lima airport, unusual things began to occur.

Many people, especially teenage girls, were looking at me in a very direct way. Later, I sat down next to a woman holding her baby. Within a few seconds, the baby was crying, with his arms outstretched for me! Have you ever seen a baby desiring to leave their mother for a complete stranger? Apparently, Alberto wasn't kidding around.

Flying back home, I asked myself,

"Okay, now you know that you are a shaman. What does that mean? What does it mean to be a shaman in the modern world?"

I certainly wasn't going to be sacrificing llama fetuses to Mother Earth with Canadians. As always, one question simply led to another.

Because our flight out of Lima was delayed, I missed my connection in Miami, which was a wonderful piece of good fortune. Thanks to the delay, I got to extend my trip one more night, going over the details of our adventures with my new American friends – even if it was at the *very mystical* Airport Howard Johnson's Restaurant.

The next morning I arrived at Miami International Airport and checked my baggage.

"March 27th," the check-in attendant said, examining my passport. "My grandmother was born on March 27th. Whenever I meet someone born on that day, I think that they must be a good person."

"Yes, they are!" I replied. The synchronicity of meeting Ligia had not been lost on the Universe.

Once home, I was on the phone to Sheena soon after.

"Sheena, I was told in Peru that I'm a shaman. What should I do now? I don't know what to do!"

"Don't do anything," she wisely advised. "Just go back to work. You've been through a lot."

Returning to the "real world" I found myself leading a double-life, more and more. All of my money would be spent on spiritual books, seminars and travel, with the hope that my efforts would eventually lead toward a much more spiritual occupation.

HEART

Soon after our trip, Ligia and I were e-mailing each other regularly. More and more, I could see that she was a person who could not only understand me, but could also identify with my perceptions. She dreamt passionately for a better world, and to play a bigger role in it, as did I. But sometimes I wondered if she could endure the trials of the mundane, daily life with the same passion. She was a marvel to dream with, but would she be a dream to live with? I wasn't sure. It's hard to pay the bills when your head is always in the clouds. Nevertheless, I visited her only four months after we met in Peru.

Weeks before my trip to Brazil, I was dreaming again…

I saw myself on a tour, overlooking São Paulo from a lush mountainside. To my right were a few trees and a small waterfall, where shirtless street kids were laughing and playing. In the distance, an endless sea of office buildings sat alongside a wide river. Overhead flew a group of giant, blue and black butterflies, each with a wingspan of about six feet.

As I watched these majestic creatures soar above us, one of them got caught in a barren, burnt tree to my left. Meanwhile, the waterfall had become a concoction of rusty plumbing under which the children were showering in filthy water. Looking down again at the city, the river was now a thick brown paste of pollution. Everything was dying.

When I awoke, the message of the dream was unmistakable. Brazil, especially São Paulo, is a city that has some of the worst environmental and social problems in the world. But, because they are so bad, it's also a place where people are working hard to resolve them. This dream stayed with me. It was as if not only Ligia was calling me, but Brazil as well.

Arriving in São Paulo, I remember the look of innocent expectation on Ligia's face the second she saw me descending the airport escalator. While I was a little nervous with the level of commitment we were moving toward, we quickly slipped into the easy vibe we felt for each other. We were clicking again. We hopped in her car and immediately headed for Rio de Janeiro.

After a few breezy days on the beach, Ligia took me to the Sambodromo to see Rio's famous Carnival parade. Feeling the deep rumble of the first samba school entering the packed stadium, I had goose bumps from head to toe. Approaching us from the right was a mad passion the likes of which I'd never seen. I'd caught a small glimpse of such a thing late into the evening at Twilight Zone, my old haunt, but thousands of people like this, dancing and singing their hearts out all night? It was overwhelming.

"You could give Canada a billion dollars and it would never be able to pull off something even close to this," I told her. Here's what my life had been missing – heart.

As the first group of dancers approached, to my astonishment, I recognized them. Leading the entire Carnival were about eight men, all dressed as giant, blue butterflies with black trim. They could not have looked more like the ones in my dream. This synchronicity was not lost on Ligia. We stayed at the Sambodromo all night, leaving long after the Sun rose. I walked back to the subway with Ligia and her friends, completely inspired and utterly exhausted.

Our nine days together were stimulating, warm and easy. I felt as at home with her as I did in her relaxed, but troubled country. After recovering from Carnival, we headed south to Ilha Grande (The Big Island), a nature reserve a short boat ride from the coast.

While an intoxicating mix of sun and samba would dazzle anyone, it was our conversations that really got me: shamanism, transpersonal psychology, quantum physics, spirituality, synchronicities, values, integrity, love, sex, dreams, success, failure, insanity, our future together. Nothing was off limits – not one ounce of bullshit or fluff. Every word was important, every word was honest. Ligia was the most transparent person I'd ever met.

She also liked to back up her words with action. One afternoon on Ilha Grande, we set out for the best beach on the island, a two-hour mountain hike from our hotel. Once at the beach, we got so caught up in our own fun that we lost track of the time. The Sun was going down and all of the tour boats that took people back to town had left. Our only options for returning to the hotel were to either rent a private boat (which would have been very expensive), or hike back over the mountain in the dark.

After an hour of searching for a safer way back, Ligia said to me, "Come on, Sean. We talk about being shamans, let's start acting like it!" By then, sundown had long past.

With that, she bought a bottle of water and a candle from a bar on the beach. After drinking the water, she cut the bottle in half with a knife. She then turned the top half of the bottle upside down, using it as a make-shift candelabra, which would protect the flame from the beach breeze. After getting some directions, we hiked back over the jungle covered mountain by candlelight.

Later, Ligia confessed that she wanted to impress me. She did. Despite being university educated, there was a primal rawness about her that I'd never seen before.

For a woman full of surprises, Ligia had one more that would take our relationship to the next level.

Back when I'd first arrived home from Peru, I sent her a blank card, in which I drew an entire map of North and South America. On the map, I marked her city of São Paulo, and mine of Toronto. To the left I childishly wrote, "Ligia, you live too far away! Move closer!"

As it turns out, Ligia's sister and her family were moving to New York, where Ligia's brother-in-law was working for a Brazilian bank. The opportunity to "move closer" was actually there.

Arriving home from Brazil, I was still unsure of what the next move would be. When your girlfriend is halfway around the world, each move feels like one toward commitment or breaking up. There is no happy middle space that guys love, where you are just having sex and having fun with no particular plan. You are either moving toward or away from marriage. Yikes!

In retrospect, that's what I'd been doing anyway. I hadn't had a girlfriend for about five years, simply because I didn't want to waste my energy getting into a relationship that I would have to fight to get out of a year or two later. I guess, by default, I was ready for marriage.

The feeling Ligia left me with was a lingering one. Although I feared marriage, afraid that my feelings for her would change with time, I would find myself asking, "Do you really want to let this one go?" There was just so much to her that was unique. I think she was the first woman that I'd ever been with that was actually good for me. I was, somehow, better with her than without her.

Six months would pass before I'd see her again, but this time she was coming to stay with her sister's family, just outside of New York City. But before she got settled, I needed to take her on a little road trip. Like many Brazilians, Ligia had this idea of America as being a completely materialistic culture, and not much else. I wanted to show her that there was more to American life than that.

I booked her first night on American soil at the Luxor Hotel & Casino – the black, glass pyramid on the Las Vegas strip. Not only did I want to impress her, I also wanted to freak her out. The Luxor did just that!

Her first lesson in American life was that, yes, it is an extremely materialistic society. Las Vegas is the most money worshipping city I've ever seen. But it's also a blast! For three days we had a great time roaming monster size casinos that take the concept of "tacky" and raise it to a high art-form. We never gambled a cent.

Then I flipped the script on her, renting a motor home for a trip to Sedona, Arizona. After reading many New Age books, I was curious to see what an entire town of spiritual seekers would be like. I was also sure that Sedona would smash any stereotypes Ligia had regarding American culture.

Without a doubt, Sedona was an eye-opening experience for both of us. It actually freaked me out. While obviously very open and spiritual, I never could have envisioned a town with so many, well, flakes! One couple we met could not park their van without consulting an oracle they carried with them. Another woman claimed to be meeting space aliens out in the desert on a regular basis.

Then there were the channelers. Many of the people we met were in contact with a spirit named White Buffalo Calf Woman. The trouble is, whenever they channeled her, they all spoke in a high-pitched, squeaky voice that just cracked us up. Needless to say, Ligia found these people to be a far cry from the stereotypical Americans she'd seen on TV.

But, as open-minded as they were, was their spiritual path leading somewhere? It was in Sedona where I first realized that pushing the limits of one's spirituality could also lead you into a fantasy world almost entirely divorced from reality. If religion was "the opium of the people," then Sedona was the "crack den" of spirituality.

Leaving behind the red-rock monoliths of Sedona, we ventured into an entirely different America, the Navajo and Hopi Indian Reservations. Life there was remarkably quiet. Imagine an advertising-free, desert landscape, as far as the eye can see. And unlike the exotic shamanic seekers we had just met, the few native Indians we came across were simple, uncomplicated people.

One night, I realized that our motor home was being followed by a car through the reservation. I was a little nervous. In Canada, some of the native people carry a lot of resentment toward whites and there have been a few violent stand-offs on or near reservations. I wasn't sure how the locals would respond to us travelling through.

As the car showed no sign of passing, I finally pulled over to see what they wanted. We opened our motor home door to find a woman and her two kids. They had been out for a drive simply because they were bored. When they saw our motor home, they thought that we might be lost, or looking for a place stay. We invited them in and talked for about an hour! The woman invited us to stay at their house for the night, but we politely declined. She was just excited to meet people from off the reservation. For her, we were the night's entertainment.

We also visited Oraibi, a Hopi village which is the oldest continuous settlement in North America. As we walked into town from the highway, we passed a sign saying, "No Photographs." The settlement was basically a few very simple houses, a couple of broken down trucks, some old farming equipment and not much else. It felt like a ghost town, not a soul in sight.

"I feel like we are being watched," I told Ligia, even though I didn't see anyone around. We continued to explore the area.

"NO PHOTOGRAPHS!" a woman shouted from one of the houses. Sure enough, I turned to see that Ligia had her camera out. That's the thing about Brazilians. All rules are meant to be broken. Ligia was no exception.

Arriving at the Grand Canyon, we had one major concern – parking. Months earlier, I had tried to reserve a hook-up for the motor home on the park grounds. No use. Little did I know, spaces there were booked up to six-months in advance. As a result, we started to strategize as to where we might find parking, hours before we got there. If we were lucky, I hoped to find a place a few miles from the park.

At the outside chance that something might be free, we pulled into the only motor home facility on the park grounds.

"You are not going to believe this," said the attendant. "We just had one family pull out of their reservation ten minutes ago. You're timing is perfect."

No reservation and we were parked a two-minute walk from the canyon. Awesome!

Approaching the South Rim for the first time, we came across a large crowd of people sitting on a nearby slope. Everyone was looking west, as if they were waiting for a movie to begin. We soon realized what all the fuss was about. With rays of light flooding the canyon, the sunset here was the most spectacular I'd ever seen. Once the Sun had graced us with its marvelous performance, the whole audience applauded and whistled. I only wish there had been an encore.

The same could be said for our tour together, "Encore! Encore!" Each day brought us closer together until, in the end, we were feeling like a real couple. Our last night on the road, we parked the motor home across from Lake Mead, just outside of Las Vegas. Star-gazing on the roof of our vehicle, we sent prayers of gratitude to the Spirits for our memorable two weeks together. In keeping with a tradition we learned from the Inca, we closed our journey by spraying alcohol, in this case ZIMA, into each other's faces.

"Ho!"

Once Ligia settled in at her sister's house in Chestnut Ridge, New York, I would drive down from Toronto about once a month. Then at Christmas, we went to California together, driving from San Francisco to Santa Barbara. Everywhere we went, we lived it up and had a ball. Spend, spend, spend!

During that time, it would have been easy for anyone to criticize my "pseudo jet-setting" lifestyle as completely immature. Being over thirty and still living at home, I was driving my parents crazy. They simply couldn't understand why I would blow all of my money travelling instead of moving into my own apartment. However, for me, "investing" in these trips with Ligia was simply something that needed to be done.

I had an insatiable need to show her all of the interesting cities of the United States. In fact, I wanted to show them to myself as well. For most of my life I'd wanted to live in the U.S. and truly experience America. With Ligia or without, between the ages of thirty and thirty-five I found myself in all of the major American cities that I'd wanted to know. Sometimes I felt as if I were living at the airport – and loving it!

One weekend we headed to Atlantic City, where we would stay at the Trump Taj Mahal. The fact that we were visiting another casino city was not lost on Ligia.

"Sean, what is going on with you and these casinos? I mean, you don't even gamble."

"I don't know," I replied. I was just drawn to them.

Ironically, the one place we didn't visit was Toronto. Once in the United States, Ligia simply couldn't get the Canadian visa. The closest we got was the time we met in Niagara Falls. From the American side of Lake Ontario, she could catch a glimpse of the Toronto skyline in the distance.

As we got to know each other, I always came away from our encounters feeling better than I actually thought I would. The inevitable burst of our romantic bubble never arrived. We kept asking ourselves when our trip to Peru was going to end. It never really did.

One Saturday afternoon, we made plans to visit a variety of sites in Manhattan. The Guggenheim was closed. Tavern-on-the-Green had a private party. MOMA was being renovated. All day we marched across the city in the cold rain. The day should have been a disaster, but it wasn't. We were having a fabulous time wandering from one disappointment to the next. We finished the day having a bland meal at the Hard Rock Cafe, soaking wet. The day was so bad, we couldn't help but laugh.

"If I'm having fun with Ligia on a day like today," I thought, "maybe we've got a shot."

After a few months of travelling here and there, we would start to build a life together.

AMBITION

While Ligia and I were enjoying our long distance romance, I was still struggling with what to do about my career. Whether to hang on to advertising until something more spiritual showed up, or to simply let go and hope for a miracle, was a major dilemma. At least this time my frustrations were not due to a lack of success.

On one project, David and I were testing three commercials for a major American bank whose ad agency was based in San Francisco. As I'd done most of the work, he asked me to fly out there with him in order to help organize the material for what would be a two hour presentation.

A business trip with the boss to San Francisco was a huge deal for me at the time. Considered a special city by most, it was revered by account planners as it had earned a reputation for being the best place in America to work, in our profession. The agencies there were famously creative and innovative. Before my awakening, I'd dreamed of one day working there myself.

Unfortunately, even on the most exciting business trip of my career, my soul was still gnawing at me. The in-flight movie was *Jerry Maguire.* As I watched Tom Cruise strut from meeting to meeting, cell-phone in hand, I couldn't help but think, "There I am, Jerry Maguire. How much longer for this fake life?"

Mind you, a glass of wine with the boss at the St. Francis Hotel and a stretch limo ride to our morning meeting helped me forget my woes, if only for a few days.

As most people do, I stuck with what was comfortable and tried to improve things. I also decided that if I wasn't going to live out my current dreams, I could at least put a few of the older ones to rest. The first was to work in the United States.

From the time I was twenty, when I skipped my first Canadian winter to live in Australia, I vowed that I would move south one day. "Six winters," I would tell myself, while freezing my way from class to class at the University of Toronto, "Six winters and I'm out of here."

Regularly visiting Ligia in New York made me feel as if I were almost there. I had this idea that the more time I spent in the U.S., the closer I was to actually making the move permanent.

For six months I was in conversation with headhunters across America, looking for a solid account planning job south of the border. While my experience was rather thin at less than three years as a planner, I did have something to brag about.

The first project I ever did for WeCU led to the creation of an award winning ad campaign for Campbell's Soup. The ideas for these commercials stemmed directly from insights I'd discovered while conducting in-home research. Ironically, the agency behind the campaign was OMNI, my old agency.

There were a few prospects out there, but nothing quite right. By February of 1999, Ligia was getting impatient. Living with an unclear future in the New York winter was wearing on her. Finally, one job came up through two different headhunters. Apparently, few planners were interested in it because it was in the advertising backwater of... Las Vegas.

The main client of this agency was Mandalay Resort Group, owners of the Luxor.

"The Luxor!" I thought. "Casinos!" That was the job for me.

Ligia and I would return to where her trip to America had started. From a research and strategy point of view, I loved the idea of working there. While other planners turned their noses at the idea of working in such an insignificant advertising market, I relished the thought of investigating the seedy allure of the casino business.

Plus, could there be any place more spiritual? Just kidding. Looking back, while I may not have been mentally ill, I certainly did have split-personality disorder.

However, after my first phone interview with the agency in Las Vegas, I once again had reservations about staying in the business. After discussing it with Sheena, I actually called Ligia and proposed the idea of simply dropping everything and moving to Brazil with her, right away. Ligia talked me out of it, saying that we should get to know each other a little better before making that move. I reluctantly agreed.

The next day, Ligia called and said that she had changed her mind, but by then she'd already convinced me to go to Vegas!

The salary for the move would be equal to $100,000 Canadian dollars. I'd been out of the hospital for about three years and already tripled my salary. That "mental illness" of mine was obviously paying off.

A new job, a new city, a new girlfriend, a new SUV, a new apartment. Could anything else have changed? Somehow, I doubt it.

Living in Las Vegas had its ups and downs. While Ligia and I were having a ball, I think I probably spent a little too much time with her and not enough time at work. It felt more like we were on an extended honeymoon. In fact, it became just that, as we were married on January 1st, 2000, about seven months after moving in together. And where to honeymoon when you already live in Las Vegas? Hawaii, of course! We spent two weeks in Oahu and Maui, where I introduced Ligia to my favorite islands.

The Vegas job didn't last long. The president of the agency and I didn't exactly hit it off. While doing his best to appear friendly and politically correct, he had the underlying personality of a mob boss. After a few months of working there, it was pretty clear that things were not going to work out.

I should have known I was in trouble from the beginning. One evening, I was with some of my new colleagues, casually watching a focus group from the backroom. Jane, the V.P. who hired me, called me over to ask for a "favor."

"Sure, what is it?" I replied, eager to please.

"Would you be able to go to a shareholders meeting at one of our clients tomorrow?"

"Of course," I said. "What for?'

"When you arrive, there will be a guy at the door who will give you a question."

"A question?" I asked, somewhat lost.

"Yes, a question on a piece of paper. At some point during the press conference, if our client is being asked a question by the media that they don't want to answer, you will be signaled to ask your question, which our client will then answer."

"Oh, okay. I guess that's fine," I replied, perplexed by her request.

I sat down by the one-way glass, watching the focus group unfold, when the implications of what I'd just agreed to do started to sink in. I was to be the agency's bitch.

After a few minutes, I returned to Jane's side.

"Jane, I'm sorry, but I can't do this."

"Why not?" she warmly asked.

"I think it's completely unethical."

"Why? It's a free country. Anyone can be there, and anyone can ask whatever they want!"

It sounded like such a pre-programmed answer.

"And the press has the right to ask whatever they want," I said.

"Okay, no problem," she replied, with a guarded smile.

Now, I can't say that I was finished with the agency after that day, but the relationship never became what I would call, warm. They made me nervous, and I think I made them nervous.

Shortly after returning from our honeymoon in Hawaii, Jane let me know that they were less than satisfied.

Ironically, while the powers-that-be were unhappy with my work, our clients at Mandalay Resort Group had been quite pleased. I had the opportunity to do research and strategic planning on three of their casinos: Luxor, Excalibur and Circus Circus. On a personal level, it was in working on those casinos that I got the most satisfaction; not because of any great advertising campaign that came out of my work, but because of how much I learned about Americans themselves.

Each casino catered to a different type of person. Luxor focused on upper-middle class, urban customers. The Excalibur was a hot-spot for "Middle America" – farmers and small town people. Finally, Circus Circus targeted lower-income groups and Hispanics from California. It was an amazing experience of contrasts, seeing how these different groups think and feel; how they responded to research techniques and different styles of advertising, and the variety of ways in which they expressed themselves.

It was surprising to see how highly educated people were so much more open and imaginative than those with less education. During one session, two young women walked out of our interview because they were actually afraid of my projection exercises.

Using image cards that came from a type of tarot deck, I would ask people to select pictures that reminded them of the hotel in which they were staying. These two ladies feared my deck of cards, thinking that I was using them for some kind of occult practice. I just wanted them to show me pictures that reminded them of the hotel!

In contrast, one marketing guy I spoke with spread out about thirty different cards relating to his stay at the Luxor, and had an interesting point to make regarding each card. This contrast in consciousness was a valuable learning experience that would have implications well into the future.

With about four months left on my one-year contract, Ligia and I realized that the best move for us would be to visit Brazil, to meet her entire family for the first time. The only problem was, I didn't have the money to pay for the kind of extended trip I wanted to take. As a result, I started looking for another account planning job, this time in the city of my dreams, San Francisco.

Ligia wasn't thrilled with this idea as she hadn't been home for two years.

"Sean, you've got to get a freelance job!" she told me. When she first mentioned it, I thought it would be impossible. First, I was on a work visa for employment at one company; second, I'd never done a freelance job in my life, and third, where would I get one? Las Vegas was a tiny advertising market.

As it turns out, getting a freelance job is exactly what happened. With two months left on my contract, I accepted a project with my agency's archrival, effectively doubling my salary for my last two months in Las Vegas. With that extra income, we were able to plan a trip to Brazil for six months!

If by now you are getting the impression that my life had become one easy cruise where I could travel endlessly, somehow having the income to pay for whatever it was

I desired; where opportunities presented themselves at every turn, making all of my dreams come true, you would not be mistaken. While my journey had many twists and turns, it also felt like I was moving through a dream of my own creation. After coming up with the money to travel Brazil, I was feeling like anything was possible.

INTENSITY

Our return journey to Brazil was not a simple sight-seeing tour. It was also my first tentative attempt at escaping from advertising. I figured, if I was ever going to get out of that game, Brazil would probably become my new home. But before I decided to move in, I wanted to see as many "rooms" as possible.

From the minute Ligia and I arrived, we were travelling non-stop, first visiting family and friends in the state of São Paulo, then on a four-month backpacking expedition to the northeast and the Amazon.

Getting to know Ligia's entire family for the first time, I was pleased to find a distinct lack of drama. Her parents had the same rock-solid foundation to their marriage that I'd grown up with. Her brother's family was a very close-knit group. I'd never seen two sisters get along so well as Ligia's nieces, Ana and Eliana. There was never a bad word between them.

There was only one problem. I couldn't figure out how Ligia got to be, well...*Ligia*. She was the most passionate, adventurous person I'd ever met. Her family was the opposite. Always leaning toward caution, they were an entirely pragmatic, conservative clan. Was there some special "engineering" gene in the family DNA that Ligia had missed out on? Perhaps.

The mystery would only be solved once we visited Ligia's university friends in Santos, a port city on the coast. Mostly composed of psychologists and social workers that had remained close for decades, meeting them I felt like the *Summer of Love* had never really ended. Sure, now they were all in their forties, even fifties, but you would never know it. They partied like they were still in college!

There was a lot to adjust to, no doubt about that. Sleeping in Ligia's parents' house, I would find St. Teresina watching over us from a painting above the headboard. Let's just say it dampened the mood a little.

Whenever I'd spoken to Canadians or Americans about my upcoming trip, they would always tell me to watch out for the crime in Brazil. Why didn't anyone warn me about the doorframes?

Brazilians in the northeast, or *nordestinos*, are not exactly built like the wispy supermodels for which the country is famous. Nope, these folks are just plain short. So short, that their doorways are often less than six feet high. Being six-foot two, I smashed my head into a doorframe about once a day. I eventually started wearing a baseball cap for protection. The worst was when I would bend over to walk through and *still* bump my head – those were the ones that really hurt. So, if you ever visit the northeast of Brazil, don't worry about the crime, it's the doorframes that might kill you.

The most adventurous part of our journey began in the port city of Belém, at the mouth of the Amazon River. Boarding a crowded ferry there, Ligia and I spent the next month exploring the river basin, eventually arriving at the city of Manaus, in the heart of the rainforest.

With a capacity of well over one-hundred people, the ferry was not the politically correct eco-tour you might imagine. With local music blasting, the top deck was one non-stop party where the guys guzzled beer all day and the few single women on board had their dance cards full. With the booze flowing and socializing endless, Ligia was working overtime as my interpreter just to keep me in the conversation.

One floor below was another open-air deck where we found parents resting in their hammocks, watching over their playing children. For most, privacy was non-existent as their "cabin" was a pair of hammock hooks and a small space on the floor for their belongings. Initially, Ligia and I opted for one of the few private rooms available, but as we got more comfortable, we realized that the air was better among the masses. It was also more fun!

Still trying to protect my sensitive skull, the only time I took off my cap was during lunch, when the ship's captain would insist that I remove it before dining. I suppose one moment of respect was necessary before we battled the other passengers for our rice, black beans and roasted chicken.

Normally, the voyage to Manaus would take five days, but we chose to take our time, spending two weeks exploring the adjacent Tapajós River as well. It was there that we had some of our most memorable adventures.

Stepping off the ferry in Santarém, about half-way to Manaus, I was instantly seduced by the rustic riverboats docked at the town's pier. Simple wooden structures, usually painted white, with red or blue trim, their design had remained unchanged since the French opened up the area to rubber barons over a century earlier.

After a few days in town, enjoying the creature comforts of civilization, we boarded one of these smaller vessels with our newly discovered guide, Ari. For the next few weeks he escorted us to secluded villages found along the Tapajós. A young, good-looking guy, Ari was a true sailor – a woman in every port! At least he came by it honestly, as his dad had fathered twenty-two children.

My *Canadian-ness* left me feeling a little sheepish as we would arrive at people's homes completely unannounced. But everywhere we went, the villagers were eager to meet us and invite us into their world. Living in these isolated areas of limited opportunity, anything that breaks the routine is welcome. Usually they would take us on a tour of the nearby jungle, then we'd have lunch together.

One afternoon, seeing the day's catch on the table, Ligia asked, "Does this fish taste good?"

"All fish tastes good when you're hungry," replied our host. Being an older farmer, I could see that there was experience behind his words. At some point, most of the people in these villages had known hunger. During the dry season, the waters would be low and the fish, easy prey, as they had no place to hide. But during the rainy season the river rose ten to twenty feet higher. With so much more space, the fish became more difficult to catch and meals harder to come by.

One day we arrived at the home of Ari's cousin who was about to go fishing. Armed with a short spear attached to a black rubber band, and a dive mask, we watched as he jumped into the shallows near his home.

Seconds later, he surfaced with a punctured fish that looked like a large piranha. After playing spectator for a while, I was invited to give the spear-fishing a try. Always comfortable in the water, I jumped in.

Have you ever tried to shoot an arrow under the water? It's impossible. I couldn't even stand on the bottom long enough to point the spear in *any direction*, let alone at a fish. Of course, by then, I couldn't breathe either and had to come up for air. I was a disaster.

Fortunately, my frantic splashing around provided great entertainment for Ari and Ligia. At least I was good for something.

Docking our boat that night, the sound of the wind howled through the air.

"Wait a second. I hear the wind, but I don't feel anything? What's happening?" I thought.

"The monkeys," Ari explained. What I'd heard was not the wind at all, but a large band of monkeys in the nearby forest.

The sounds of the jungle would continue to enchant me. Long after Ligia and Ari were asleep in their hammocks, I was awake listening to the echoes of bullfrogs rippling across the water.

"This is so cool."

Unlike the ferry, there was no shower on this boat. Bathing meant jumping into the Coca-Cola colored river. No, it wasn't black from pollution, but from the jungle foliage, like a river full of tea leaves. Being so dark, it was impossible to see if there were any predators nearby – snakes, piranha, alligators, stingray. Was it dangerous? Sure. It's the Amazon.

This first leg of our journey was a real test, as I knew it would be. Months earlier, I was having a recurring dream,

"I'm hiking through the jungle when, in front of me, I see that my path is interrupted by a shallow creek. On the other side is a muddy slope which I'll need to climb. What shoes should I wear? Sandals would slip, tennis shoes would get soaked, hiking boots would be ruined."

On a deeper level, I knew what the dream was really about. I was still confused about my direction in life, looking for my purpose. The various footwear represented different roles for me in society, but there was no clear answer to what that role should be. I never could decide what shoes to wear.

On a not-so-deep level, I just had a thing about my feet. All my life they had been protected by immaculate, white sweat socks and a clean pair of sneakers. The soles of my feet were baby-soft, sensitive and callous-free. While I'm sure they looked fine to everyone else, to my soul, they were a disappointment. My feet had never really *lived*. My soles had no soul.

Hmmmm. That was deeper than I thought.

Near the end of our time on the Tapajós, my soles got a chance to prove themselves. Ari had taken Ligia and me close to a remote village far down-river, where the people were almost pure Indian.

Once off the boat, to get to the village we needed to walk across a swampy mud-flat, dotted with trees. With the Sun above, getting across was a little tricky, but manageable, as we could get our footing on roots and rocks along the way.

Arriving at the village, the locals welcomed us in a surprisingly formal manner, introducing us to their culture by having the children perform one of their traditional dances. After sunset, however, the mood became more relaxed as Ligia and I amused them with stories of our adventures.

While our evening there was an enjoyable one, returning to the boat was another story. The tide had risen to the point where the mud-flat had become submerged. The locals told us that when the tide is high they paddle across in a dug-out canoe, but at that moment, the water wasn't deep enough. We needed to walk through the swamp.

While Ligia and Ari crossed without much of a fuss, for me, every move felt perilous. Stepping into the squishy mud-soup, it was impossible to use any form of footwear. I simply had to dip my virgin toes into the goo. Especially now that the tide had risen, this swamp was full of spiders, frogs and a myriad of other creatures; any of which I could step on.

Waiting on the other side, Ligia and Ari shouted advice on which path to take across the mud. With their encouragement, I nervously toddled my way forward.

"Congratulations! I know how difficult that was for you!" Ligia said, hailing my arrival.

My soul was proud. So were my soles.

The few tourists we met along the way were mostly nature enthusiasts. With their gigantic cameras, they painstakingly waited for that perfect moment when they could capture the wildlife of the Amazon at its finest.

As for me, I just liked to push stuff. With my basic Portuguese, conversation was slow and difficult, but if there was anything around that needed a good shove, I was a giant among mere mortals.

The morning after my victorious swamp walk, the tide was so low that we couldn't get our boat off the shore. For over two hours the village men and I worked to get Ari's boat back into the river. Eventually, we devised a strategy using a couple of wooden beams for extra leverage. We all cheered as we finally got the boat off the beach. It was a real team effort.

By then I had gotten used to being called on for the heavy work. One night, heading to a beach house near Belém, Ligia hired a guy with a donkey cart to take us along the beach to our destination. Little did we know, the donkey didn't like water. Approaching a creek-bed, he came to a dead stop. With the owner pulling hard on the reins, Ligia and I pushed the cart across the creek, getting the donkey moving in the right direction.

"*Vai! Vai! Vai!*" is what Brazilians shout when they need to push something. It means, "Go! Go! Go!" I found that out the time we took a local bus to a farm in Maranhão, one of the poorest regions of the country. Along the way, the dirt road had disintegrated into pure sand. The bus could get no traction at all. Eventually, everyone onboard needed to get out and help push the bus through the sand. Until that time, I never knew people could actually push a bus through *anything*.

Everywhere we went, Ligia and I sought out shamans in the hope of finding some clue to our elusive spiritual vocation. The most interesting shaman we met was a street vendor in downtown Manaus. Having left his tribe for the city, he now made his living peddling the tools of his trade. Like a pharmacist handing out medications, he would sell the various ingredients required for the ritual you needed to do to solve your problem. A concoction of honey, herbs and alcohol would probably be enough to satisfy the spirits for a simple healing, but I'm sure the alligator skull in the back was for something a little more serious.

We bonded with him right away, hanging around his stand for a good part of the afternoon. When I asked him why he chose to live in the city, he rubbed his fingers together, "Money!" Just like anyone else, a guy's gotta make a buck.

Before we left, he gave us each a coconut ring for protection, something we would both wear for the rest of our trip.

We also consulted a female shaman who lived in a small Indian village a few hours from Manaus. Usually, I find shamans fascinating, but upon entering her dwelling, it was a few of her family members that first caught our attention. Sitting next to her were a girl and boy, both about fourteen years old. The girl was holding a baby, that Ligia assumed was her little sister. As it turns out, these two kids had been married for over a year and the baby was their child! Things were definitely different in the Amazon.

In order to help us find our spiritual purpose, the shaman recommended doing a purification ritual with a special bath water that she had mixed. I was reluctant, as the price was around R$30, but it was something Ligia felt we needed to do.

More and more, Ligia's sincerity in seeking out our mission revealed itself. After a few minutes of speaking with the shaman, she started to cry. Their conversation had provided her with a sense of relief. The shaman had validated Ligia's intuitions that we were on the right track.

That night we stayed in an utterly surreal hotel, the Ariau Amazon Towers. A three hour ferry ride from Manaus, the entire hotel sits on thirty-foot stilts – tall enough to stay above the river during the rainy season. One of the main features of the hotel is a narrow, mile-long boardwalk through the canopy. For better or for worse, using the boardwalk through the jungle felt wonderfully civilized.

Catering mostly to foreign tourists, hotel rooms there were a little out of our range. Fortunately, they did have a camping facility where we could hang our hammocks. As no tours had been reserved, we were lucky enough to have the entire space to ourselves. A completely original structure, the facility looked like a six-floor, open-air loft, with a central staircase that had been built around a massive tree. For breakfast, we climbed the stairs to a tree-house at the top, overlooking the endless jungle canopy.

The hotel was full of bizarre oddities. Along the board-walk, we discovered a glass pyramid full of fake plants and meditation pillows. Being the spiritual hub of the hotel, Ligia and I were naturally drawn to it (the air-conditioning didn't hurt either).

Then there was the UFO landing site. According to an employee we met there, the owner was an eccentric middle-aged man with a fourteen year-old girlfriend. Not only did he believe in UFOs but he was convinced that if he built a landing site for them, the aliens would arrive. What he designed was an area that looked a lot like a helicopter pad, with a "Welcome" sign painted in many languages. One night, he had a team of staff members stay with him at the landing site until dawn, as he was convinced that his beloved space aliens would finally appear. Needless to say, the evening was a bit of a let-down.

The hotel also had one *not-so-fabulous* attraction. Around midnight, the fruit bats in the area enjoyed playing the game, "Scare the crap out of the tourist."

Because the entire hotel was thirty feet in the air, the only way to walk from one place to another was to use the boardwalk. It was there that the bats liked to hang out. Flying only four or five feet above the boardwalk, they had a habit of coming straight at you, until they detected you with their sonar. Then, about one foot from your face, they would veer off, avoiding collision.

"Jesus Christ! Jesus Christ!" I shouted, wiping their flapping wings away from my ears. Ligia howled at my sudden return to Christianity. Mind you, she wasn't crazy about those bats either. The only way to make it through was to keep your head down with your hands over your eyes.

Before checking out of our trippy pad, we ventured to the far end of the hotel grounds for our sacred bath. After stripping naked, the two of us stepped into the river. Raising the two-liter bottle of blessed bathwater, I ceremoniously poured it over Ligia's head. She then did the same for me. Just as we were about to close our ritual, we were hit with a powerful thunderstorm.

"Wooohoooooo!" we shouted, as the hard rain pelted our skin. We may not have found our purpose just yet, but we were A-L-I-V-E!

Twenty nights of sleeping in hammocks, bathing in the river and fighting off insects had left Ligia and me with a craving for simple hedonistic pleasure. So, from Manaus we flew back to the resort city of Fortaleza, on the Atlantic coast. We spent the next few weeks visiting the picturesque beach towns of the northeast – mostly places you can't pronounce, like *Jericoacoara*.

As with most beach vacations, we had a fabulous time, but there wasn't a whole lot to write about. Somehow, comfort and adventure rarely go hand in hand.

Drying off from the beach, we headed for Salvador, my favorite city of our tour. There, we witnessed our first Candomblé ceremonies. Held in the humble homes of the hillside favelas which engulf the city, we respectfully watched as practitioners worked themselves into trances, channeling the African Orixá spirits which they worshiped. While it was clear that these people were poor and uneducated, it was also obvious to me that they knew something we modern folk had long forgotten. There was power in their trance states. Power to do what? I wasn't sure.

During one ceremony, we saw a teenage girl trying to dance herself into a trance, but her inhibitions were getting in the way. Little by little, the woman leading the Candomblé session would lean over to her, whispering gentle encouragement.

Finally, after about twenty minutes, the girl slipped into the bongo player's hypnotic rhythms. As her head dropped and shoulders swayed, she let out a sudden, primal shriek. The group leader leaped over to her in excitement. The girl had done it! She had broken through to the Other Side. The elder then embraced the girl with warmth and support.

Witnessing this moment, I recalled my own experience on the Other Side, and how it had been so grossly misunderstood by those around me. And yet, these simple people – they definitely had some idea. I would have been much better off with them than I was in the hospital. I left the ceremony deeply moved.

One morning I was perusing the local newspaper, looking for something to do. I wasn't having much luck, as my Portuguese was still terrible. What do I see in the events section, but a small ad for a lecture by Dr. Stan Grof at the University of Bahia.

Wanting Ligia to see him in the flesh, we attended the event that night. For me, his speech was a bit of a let-down as it was identical to one he gave at the holotropic breathwork seminar I'd attended in Vermont a few years earlier. At the break, though, I had the opportunity to speak with

Dr. Grof personally, thanking him for the impact that his books had on my life. That certainly made the evening worthwhile.

I had a feeling that we would meet someone in our travels that would completely surprise us. I never imagined it would be Dr. Stan Grof.

Our journey took us to sixteen cities, seven national parks and two islands. It was an experience of this vast and varied country that few Brazilians will ever have. Most of our friends in São Paulo would shudder at the idea of sleeping in hammocks for a month on the Amazon River. I think I was bitten by every possible ant and mosquito known to man. We encountered poisonous snakes, tarantulas, piranhas, bats, water buffalo and drunken villagers. I also got into a few blow-ups – one with a rather territorial parrot, and another with a very cheeky monkey. Nobody steals my beer.

In spite of the difficulties, our adventure was, obviously, unforgettable. We had immersed ourselves in some of the most breathtaking, untouched landscapes on the planet. Our taste of local culture was always at the street level, never a pasteurized tourist imitation. And let's not forget the Brazilians themselves. Everywhere we went, we were treated like long-lost relatives. My apparently "hilarious" accent was always the talk of the town.

Any remnants of my comfortable suburban upbringing were gladly stripped away. I even earned myself a few calluses! Looking at our photos, I sometimes catch myself asking, "Was that really us?"

However, while we had accomplished everything we had hoped for, the spiritual mission we were seeking proved elusive. I'm not exactly sure what it was we were looking for, but whatever it was, it didn't show its face. After seven straight months of travel, I was about $5,000 in debt and could only think of one thing – getting back to work.

SELL-OUT

With an exciting expedition to Brazil to brag about, I had no doubt that I would be able to enter the market again, finally landing that "big" advertising job that I thought might satisfy me. There was only one problem. The idea of achieving my old dream of working in San Francisco left me less than enthused.

The people I'd met in Brazil were warm and unpretentious. Reflecting on the image conscious executives that I was forced to work with in advertising, I would sink, just a little.

Over the years, I would have a recurring dream that, I think, says it all:

"I see myself alone on one side of a glass wall, staring at a group of ad-people, all sleek and sophisticated, apparently having a wonderful time. Whether they were socializing or working, it looked like a lot of fun. Soon, I'm inside the room with them, trying to fit in, trying to belong. To my disappointment, I find myself still feeling lonely, isolated and completely uninterested in what they are doing. In a sense, I want to be accepted by an exclusive club that, honestly, repulses me."

Year after year I would have similar feelings to these. But, like in a bad marriage, I kept thinking, "This time, it will be different."

By the time I got back from Brazil in February of 2001, the entire advertising market was reeling from the collapse of the "dot-coms" a few months earlier. Overnight, the Internet boom had come to a crashing halt, taking half of the ad agencies in San Francisco down with it. A few places I'd interviewed with less than a year earlier were now out of business.

Fortunately, all was not lost. Despite a tightening market I was able to arrange interviews at agencies in Los Angeles and Miami, receiving two lucrative job offers.

Within two months, I was moving to Miami to work for OCEAN Advertising and was excited to do so. Unlike the agency in Las Vegas, OCEAN had earned a reputation for doing highly creative advertising, supported by award winning account planning. At the interview, Ted, the director of account planning, seemed keen to do the kind of on-the-street, guerrilla-style research that I enjoyed and found to be very effective. Their client roster wasn't bad either. They had just landed the account for BMW's newly launched MINI Cooper, which I was to start working on right away. I accepted Ted's offer, even though it was for $10,000 less than the job in L.A.

"Finally, this would be the agency where I could make my mark!" At least I kept telling myself that.

By the end of my *first week* at OCEAN, I was calling the headhunter that had hooked me up with the position.

"Do you think the position in L.A. is still available?" I asked her. I was already feeling that I'd made a huge mistake.

My first day on the job, I was in a meeting with Ted and three young, uptight female executives. As I was to learn, they had a problem with the new campaign for their client, "TRUTH," Florida's teen anti-smoking organization. Previously, OCEAN had become renowned for making a series of breakthrough ads for this client, and had won prestigious account planning awards in the process.

Little did I know that the relationship between the agency and the client had taken a turn for the worst. The teenage staff at "TRUTH" was unhappy with their latest campaign and wanted it taken off the air. After watching the ads during the meeting, I could understand why our client was so upset. The ads sucked. They were far too childish for a teen audience.

"Why don't we test the ads?" Ted, my boss, suggested. "We'll make sure they come out okay."

"What? What did THAT mean?" I thought to myself. *"We'll make sure they come out okay?"*

As it turns out, that's exactly what we did.

Over the next few months, I stood by and watched as Ted devised a rather biased research project to prove that the advertising was good. He then had the results interpreted by people that would give it all a positive spin. The strongly negative comments kids said to me during focus groups were completely ignored. In essence, we were lying to the "TRUTH" kids.

While I remained patient, hoping that this was just a one-time incident, I eventually came to realize that my job as an account planner at OCEAN would be to make sure that all of the research *"came out okay."* At the very least, it was my job to go out and prove what the agency was already thinking. If anything came back negative or even different, it was shelved.

I'd always known that there was a lot of bullshit in advertising, but somehow I'd managed to maintain my own sense of integrity through it all. But this time, there would be no escape. If I was going to be accepted as part of "the team" I needed to start playing ball. By keeping me out of the loop on a number of high profile projects, Ted sent that message, loud and clear.

After work, Ligia and I would take a dip in the ocean, steps from our rented South Beach condo. Wading over a pristine, turquoise sand bar, an apparent paradise, I would repeatedly ask her, "What am I going to do? I'm in Hell!"

After four months, I had seen enough. One morning, I stood alone in the stairwell of the agency. With my hands gripping the railing, I realized that the moment of truth had come. I had a choice to make. I could go back to my desk, shut up and "play the game" like everyone else, or go up the stairs to Ted's office, tell him exactly what I thought of him and be fired.

I imagined myself five years into the future, working in San Francisco as a successful Director of Account Planning, yet with a few extra wrinkles from the lies I'd told to get there. I imagined how difficult it would be for me to look at myself in the mirror, knowing that I'd become a phenomenal success by being a huge sell-out.

Heart pounding, I shot up the stairs and sat down in Ted's office. Within a few minutes, it was over.

"You are not a planner, Ted," I calmly told him. My words definitely struck a chord as this otherwise cold and emotionless person shuddered in the light of unblinking truth.

By 10:30 a.m. I was back in our spacious, beachfront apartment, crying on Ligia's shoulder. I had just destroyed my career.

After all of this, you might think, "Great! Now Sean and Ligia can go to Brazil and he can finally end this advertising nonsense." The trouble was, by that time I was still in a bit of debt and just couldn't come to grips with the idea of moving to Brazil owing money.

I kept hanging on. I'd made a few connections in Miami with some freelance ad people that I actually liked, and did some work with them for free, just to prove myself. We hit it off and were actually planning to make a proposal to a major fitness chain together.

"Hey, maybe I'm not dead yet!" I thought.

Then came September 11th.

Roaming the streets of South Beach for the next few days, it was eerie to know what everybody was thinking, but not saying – as if the entire nation's mother had died. The grief was staggering.

Not surprisingly, along with the World Trade Centers, the advertising market came crashing down as well. The proposal to the fitness chain was put on hold, permanently.

Refusing to give up hope, we stuck around Miami for a few months, waiting on a couple of other slim opportunities. Once those disappeared, Ligia and I packed our belongings and headed to Toronto to stay with my family until we sorted things out.

"All our dreams…gone!" Ligia cried.

DEPRESSION

Each day we drove north, the air got a little colder, the sky a little grayer, and the stark reality of our situation settled in more and more. At the border we needed to convince the immigration officer that Ligia would not be applying for permanent residency.

"We're just here to meet my family, then we'll be moving to Brazil," we told him. For a second, we looked at each other with a hint of excitement in our eyes. Could it be true? Would we really be moving to Brazil?

Arriving home, I felt like a total failure. Thirty-five years old and stuck in my parent's basement with my wife! All of our dreams had become one gigantic nightmare.

Then came the months of indecision, "Should we stay in Canada, pay off our debts, and then move to Brazil in a few years? Should we just go to Brazil in debt? Should we simply settle in Canada?" At one point I even considered the advice that my mother had been hounding me with for years, to do my MBA. Of course, that would mean living with Mom and Dad for only another three more winters!

"Was it possible that less than a year earlier Ligia and I had been celebrating New Year's Eve on Copacabana Beach? What happened to my adventurous new life?"

Each morning, I would wake up in that basement, dreading the day to come. "Oh my God, we're still here," I would think to myself.

I was also angry. While it would be easy for others to criticize my decisions, for me, each choice was a sign of faith. I was trusting my intuition on a level that most would never dare. I'd been living from the heart, true to my integrity. To end up back in my parent's house left me feeling betrayed. God had abandoned me.

Most days I didn't want to see anybody. One afternoon I was at the mall when, from a distance, I recognized an old girlfriend working in one of the shops. I turned the corner before she saw me. I felt so humiliated, like every decision I'd ever made was a mistake.

Except for one.

Ligia remained supportive the entire time. She never criticized me once or tried to persuade me to move to her homeland. I knew she was dying for us to cut our losses and head south, but she also knew that the decision on what to do with my life needed to come from me. In truth, I also knew that if we settled in Canada, she would eventually divorce me. Living in Toronto, I would never be the man she married, or the man I'd hoped to be.

Occasionally, there was a small glimpse of light which helped renew my faith, just a touch. Still paying attention to my dreams, I woke up one morning with one that, at the time, made no sense at all.

"I had a dream about a koala bear," I told Ligia. What it meant, I had no idea.

Later that day, we visited a small "Psychic Fair" close to my parents' place. Held in a local public school, it wasn't exactly on the level of the Las Vegas spectacles that Ligia and I had grown accustomed to. Plus, being broke, I had no desire to part with the few dollars we had to spend.

Then I saw the koala bear.

One of the psychics had a series of photos laid out in front of her booth. Sitting in the middle of the table was one of her holding a koala bear. Even after all that we had been through, Ligia and I couldn't turn down a synchronicity like that.

"You should marry that girl," the psychic told me.

"We're already married," I replied.

"It doesn't look like you're married," she said.

"I know, it doesn't feel like we're married."

I was impressed with her immediate perception. Ligia and I felt too fresh to be married. I soon opened up about what I had gone through with advertising and how lost I felt.

"You're grieving," she told me.

"Anytime we end an important relationship in our lives, be it with a family member, a close friend or even a career, it can feel like a sort of death," she said.

It may not have been a telepathic message, but I felt validated by the psychic's insight. As I said earlier, my career was like a bad marriage. Now I was suffering through the divorce. Her words allowed me to forgive myself and be a little more patient with my feelings.

Some days were definitely worse than others. Every so often, Ligia would refer to me as the "Tatu Sean." "Tatu" is Portuguese for armadillo, a small animal that lives in a hole in the ground. Every time I would take the stairs down into our basement bedroom, I reminded Ligia of a miserable little armadillo.

"Sean, there is nothing to gain from being in that hole," she would remind me. Her encouragement gave me just enough energy to keep on going.

Mom and Dad were also very supportive. My choices had always been difficult for them to understand, so to be able to accept Ligia and me into their home for such a long period of time was commendable. It was a relief to see how well they got along – my "hippy" wife and my "fifties" parents. Underneath everything, good people are just good people, I suppose.

My year back home was a true Dark Night of the Soul, which was difficult for everybody. After eight or nine failed job interviews and about six months of part-time factory work, I finally made the decision that needed to be made all along. Ligia and I were moving to Brazil, even if we had to risk bankruptcy.

"Why don't you just steal the money," my father sarcastically suggested. I must admit, I agreed with him. I doubt there could be any greater shame to me, personally, than going bankrupt – especially after having spent so much money travelling, "chasing our dreams."

Even though bankruptcy was a very real possibility, I felt like I no longer had a choice. It was either move to Brazil or spend years in depression.

In order to set things up for my arrival, Ligia left for São Paulo in August of 2002. While she was gone, I made the preparations for selling our SUV, an Isuzu VehiCross. I'd purchased this limited edition concept vehicle when I first arrived in Las Vegas. It remains, to this day, my all-time favorite set of wheels. Returning to Toronto, I'd hoped to get over $35,000 CDN for it. Now I was prepared to sell it for anything.

Once the decision to leave had been made, my depressing year as an armadillo quickly came to a close. I was finally able to sell the VehiCross, something I'd been trying to do since we arrived. My friend Sheena had some paid work for me to do on a calendar she designs. Ligia started teaching English in São Paulo. Quite suddenly, the light came back into our lives.

A few weeks before leaving, I paid a visit to my brother and his baby son, Cameron. Whenever I'd visited them previously, Cameron had always been cautious, never engaging me in any way. Glen would tell me that he was afraid of strangers, but I never believed him. I knew I was the problem. This time, however, Cameron spent the entire afternoon on my lap, using me as his personal sofa.

I was back!

HEAVEN?

*"We must be willing to get rid of the life we've planned,
so as to have the life that is waiting for us."*
~ Joseph Campbell ~

As painful as it was to let go, I had finally destroyed my life. The decrepit Victorian house of my psyche was gone forever. I only wish I'd read Joseph Campbell's quote sooner!

Moving to São Paulo in November of 2002, I felt as if I'd abandoned my entire life history. Arriving without a plan, I had no idea of what the future might hold. It was a tremendous relief to get out of Toronto, but it was also a little scary.

Gradually, Ligia and I eased into a lifestyle that fit us very well. Her parents helped a lot, buying us a compact car and providing some money to furnish a small apartment. For the first year, we both taught English for local schools. While Ligia focused on general English, mostly with teenagers and adult beginners, I was able to earn quite a bit more money with executives. A year later, we both started teaching independently, doubling our income from the year before. By the end of our second year, we had paid off all of the debts I owed back in Canada. The bankruptcy I'd feared so much had been easily avoided.

While I originally thought that teaching English would eventually bore me, I found it to be much more stimulating than I'd imagined. It hardly felt like work at all. Once independent, I could plan my own schedule. I had no office politics or boss to deal with, plus, I was actually helping people improve their lives.

But, perhaps most importantly, I was doing something that allowed me to simply be me. I didn't have to puff myself up and act like the expert. Most classes were spontaneous, lively and a pleasure to teach. It wasn't uncommon for class to turn into a therapy session – for them, not me! Many of my students stayed with me for three or four years, and the relationships became much more like friendships than that of student-teacher.

Returning to my car after one of my first classes, I was struck by the feeling of silence within myself. No e-mails, no backstabbing, no bullshit, no drama. It was effortless. I felt free.

Basking in my newfound "retirement" as an English teacher, I also curtailed my ambitions toward that elusive spiritual work which we never could seem to find. Rather than trying to directly help others, Ligia and I focused on strengthening our own inner spirit as much as possible. In our spare time, we read what inspired us, meditated and exercised. I also got into the video game, Max Payne, for about five months. Sometimes, I just need to be a dumb guy.

One of the more interesting activities we got involved with were the shamanic rituals of an older British couple, Felicity and Andrew. We joined their group for monthly sweat lodges, which they held on their property outside of São Paulo. Then, once a year, we went to their *Sun Moon Dance,* an elaborate ceremonial retreat which involved dancing on-and-off for three days, without food and very little water. This ritual is extremely difficult to finish and requires a tremendous amount of sacrifice. But, as painful as it was, I found the intensity of the experience to be rejuvenating. It was good for my soul.

My new lifestyle didn't exactly impress anybody back home, but it felt real. After ten years of searching, I was finally living a life that was true to me.

In our third year here we decided to open our own English consulting company. For eight months we worked on a website of our own design, creating new services that we thought would appeal to executives looking to improve their English. But something funny happened. All of a sudden, everything we tried felt heavy. We often had conflicts with our webpage designers. The advertising we did on Google had less than stellar results. Managing other teachers felt tedious and draining. As it turns out, growing our own company was not inspiring at all.

To make matters worse, every once in a while, Ligia would pipe up, "Sean, you had a dream to go to Peru. You meet me there. We are born on the same day and time. We travel America, then Brazil. Then you leave everything behind to move to São Paulo so that, together, we can become…English teachers? Something is not right."

It wasn't something I wanted to hear, but I knew she had a point. So, without much fanfare, we let go of the idea of growing our company. The old me, from my twenties, would have pushed and pushed to grow my company even if it killed me. However, at thirty-nine, after all that I'd been through, I could see that what needed to die was not me, but my ego. I realized that growing my company was not something that I particularly desired, but something that I was doing in order to impress other people. I wanted to be able to say, "Yes, I moved to São Paulo with nothing and created the best English consulting firm in the city!" (Can you hear me beating on my chest? Thump, thump.) Realizing this, instead of putting more energy into our occupation, we put less.

At around the same time, Ligia's father bought us a modest, but intriguing apartment with her inheritance. Together, we would spend our time between classes over-seeing renovations and buying upgrades for our new home. We converted one of the bedrooms into a "Zen-Bahia" space, with a futon and hammock for reading, meditating, or just hanging out. We invited an artist to come in and paint a few designs on our walls and cupboard. To my surprise, the renovation became a fabulous creative outlet for both of us. By the time we were finished, every inch of our new home had our face.

Freed from any occupational ambitions and enjoying our new digs, by the end of our fourth year in Brazil I felt a profound sense of peace and happiness. I was also meditat-ing like crazy. Sitting for almost three hours at a time, it became a sort of experiment for me.

One Monday in September of 2006, I was relaxing, watching television during the afternoon. We had just spent the entire weekend with Felicity & Andrew, and about thirty members of their "tribe." It was a memorable weekend of ceremony, storytelling, and meaningful connections.

Lying there on the couch, I was overcome with a sense of gentle elation. Recognizing the unique nature of this feeling, I turned off the TV to meditate.

After about twenty minutes, Ligia came into the apartment. Seeing that I was meditating, she chose not to disturb me. A few minutes later, as I was sitting there with my eyes closed, I witnessed a brilliant flash of light.

"What is this?" I thought. "Some new spiritual level of reality I'm experiencing?"

I opened my eyes to find Ligia standing in front of me with a camera. She had just taken my picture.

"Sean, you were in bliss!" Ligia said. That's my woman. It took a few years to figure out, but one thing about Ligia is that she always knows how I'm feeling – often, before I do. It's scary.

Along with occasional moments of bliss, I'd started to reflect on something that I found to be completely baffling. I'd noticed in the biographies of famous and not-so-famous people, that many of them had a very defined idea of what they wanted to do from a young age. I suppose Tiger Woods golfing at the age of three would be the best example. Yet, despite my best efforts, I could never remember truly wanting to do *anything* for an occupation.

During university I studied economics, sociology and religion without having any desire to become an economist, sociologist or theologian. I basically fell into advertising because I enjoyed working with ideas and learning about how people think. I couldn't have cared less about the ads themselves. Teaching English, while enjoyable, was primarily a way of paying the bills and hardly what I would consider a career. In fact, the only thing I was genuinely passionate about was understanding the nature of God. But what to actually do with my acquired knowledge and experience of the spiritual realm remained a complete mystery.

Despite this sticking point, I was also very aware that the fall of 2006 was the happiest period of my adult life – not because I'd found a career, but because I'd given up looking for one. Never before had I experienced such peace and satisfaction with myself, my relationships and the world around me. After ten years of struggle, I had finally integrated my life, *by giving up*.

Based on this new self-understanding, I decided to begin 2007 with a fresh idea. Like many people, every year around New Year's Day I would write down some specific goals that I wanted to accomplish over the next twelve months. In my twenties, these goals were rarely met, as my career stagnated. After the hospitalization, however, my ability to visualize my own future became much more powerful. Yet, even with this ability, life was obviously not without its curves. Looking back, even the fulfillment of some of my most ambitious dreams had left me with a residue of dissatisfaction.

Eventually, I arrived at the idea that having no goals at all might be a lighter, more interesting way to move through life. After all, if my life was devoid of goals, perhaps it would also be free of disappointment as well. An ambition-free life may also help improve my presence in the "now," which Eckhart Tolle writes about so eloquently.

"2007 will be the year without goals!" I declared.

So, while I had intentionally devised no particular plans for the upcoming year, there would be a mission waiting for us, indeed.

Part 3

The Mission

FEAR

In April of 2007, Ligia and I got a call that would leave us both forever changed. One of our nieces was having a "crisis" and had been taken to a psychiatrist by her parents. As Ligia was conversing with her sister-in-law in Portuguese, I attempted to decipher the essential information. Over three days I would hear the symptoms: high energy level, inability to sleep, non-stop talking, taking off her blouse in front of her father, a lot of fear, etc. It sounded all too familiar.

"Ligia, I don't think Ana is having a crisis, I think she's going through what I had, a spiritual emergency."

On the following Thursday, Ligia's sister called. Apparently, Ana had been drugged out of her mind by the psychiatrist. As the story goes, she had acted very badly in front of him. Realizing what was at risk, we drove to their home the next day.

On the way up, Ligia and I devised a plan of action. From my experience in the hospital, I knew that Ana was probably extremely sensitive, and that her parents' fear of the situation would be toxic for her. It was my assumption that Ana was afraid because her parents were terrified.

"We've got to get the fear out of the house," I told Ligia.

Upon arrival, we could see that Ana had been heavily medicated. She could barely hold a glass. Nevertheless, she was outgoing and warm with us, hugging and laughing with Ligia as soon as we met her.

Right away, Ligia went upstairs with Ana to give her love and support, connecting with her as much as possible. In fact, at one point Ligia jumped in the shower with Ana, completely clothed, just to lighten the mood around what was happening.

"You're not crazy," Ligia told her. "You are going through something very, very special."

Meanwhile, I sat down with Ana's parents, sharing with them the details of my hospitalization and how beneficial the whole experience had been for my life. Despite knowing them for years now, I hadn't shared my story with Ligia's brother and sister-in-law, because I assumed, like most people, that they would be too closed-minded to understand. But, with their daughter's life in the balance, I felt I had no choice.

I told them that, if her condition was similar to mine, I thought that Ana could come out of this situation and return to a life that may be even better than before.

At first I was cautious to share my opinions because the family had been telling us how frightened Ana had been − not my experience at all. But after seeing her with Ligia for only a few minutes, it was obvious to me that she was already much more at ease. For the first time, she was able to go upstairs in her own house without someone being by her side. As time passed, I would see other symptoms similar to my own: demonstrations of strong affection toward us; a state of rapture for anything she found to be beautiful; a heightened sense of smell and hearing.

The next day, we all went to see the psychiatrist in order to get her medication reduced to a more reasonable level. In the waiting room, I watched in amazement as Ana smelled the hospital flowers. Immersing herself in their scent, it was as if they were the most beautiful she had ever seen. It all reminded me so strongly of my own experience, I felt as if I might be slipping into that mystic space myself.

By then, I'd seen enough to be sure that Ana was experiencing the same thing that I'd been through, and encouraged her parents to take her off the medication entirely.

"This is not a mental illness," I told them, "It's a spiritual emergency."

However, they chose to stick with the psychiatrist and continue with the medication for the time being.

Ligia and I stayed with them for the entire weekend. I spoke with Ana's parents for hours about my experience, the books I had read that helped me understand a spiritual emergency, what I thought was happening, and what I thought they should do. Ligia did her best to work with Ana, encouraging her to describe her feelings, express her frustrations with life and integrate what was happening into her consciousness.

As with countless seventeen year-olds, Ana had endured many changes and disappointments over the previous three months. Having recently graduated from high school, she failed to get into the University of São Paulo (USP) business program – her school of choice. As a result, while most of her friends had already moved away to other universities, she remained stuck at home. To make matters worse, her older sister and cousin had recently left for Europe on extended stays. Like a lot of girls, Ana's friendships were her life. In a matter of weeks, most of them had been stripped away.

On top of that, she was just starting to discover who she was as a person. By her own admission, Ana had spent her entire life being the "good daughter," trying to fit in and satisfy everyone else's expectations of who she was supposed to be.

One night, Ana, Ligia and I stayed up talking in the kitchen until about 5:00 a.m. At first, Ana was a little evasive, wandering here and there, speaking in a ridiculously high, babyish tone.

"Ana," I said, "I don't want to speak to this baby girl, I want to speak to the real you." She soon lowered her voice, sitting down in front of me.

"What do you want to do with your life?" I asked her.

"I don't know," she moaned.

"Let me ask you this then. How do you feel when you think about taking business courses at the University of São Paulo?"

"Hhhhhmmmm," she groaned, shoulders slumping toward the floor. Her body language could not have been more depressing.

Knowing that she had been considering the field of nutritional studies, I then asked, "Now, how do you feel when you think of nutrition?"

Arms raised above her head, she proclaimed, "When I think of nutrition, I SEE THE LIGHT!"

"Yes! Yes! That's what you need to go with! Ana, you need to follow your heart on this, or else you will never find happiness!"

By this time we were both in tears. Looking directly into each other's eyes, I could see that something essential was taking place. Our connection was strong.

"But I'm stuck with these!" she said, reaching over to the black labeled medications she was being forced to take.

"Don't worry about those," Ligia said. "We'll take care of that when the time comes."

Ligia continued to work with Ana throughout the next day, continually encouraging her to steer away from outside distractions in order to get in touch with her feelings. As we discovered, Ana had developed a bit of an Internet addiction. It was difficult to pull her away from her ultimate source of distraction, the social networking site Orkut, in order to help her become more focused. Meanwhile, I did everything I could to show her parents a less fearful way to approach their daughter's situation.

By Sunday night Ana had created a collage about how she saw herself now, and who she wanted to be in the future. In the collage she showed a strong desire to stop living life like the "baby" of the family, to mature into a young woman who embraces her femininity.

Ligia and I left Ana's house that evening feeling like we had made huge strides. In fact, we thought we may have rescued her entirely. I was expecting that her parents would take her off the medication fairly quickly.

Later in the week, Ana was taken to her psychiatrist and psychologist, both of whom said that they had never seen a girl recover so fast from her type of crisis.

Two weeks later, we saw the family again. Ana was still being medicated, but there was something refreshing about her. Her eyes revealed previously hidden depths. She told us that she had no regrets about her experience and that she felt she was, somehow, different.

"I don't care as much about what other people think," she told us.

Her father, however, was more reluctant. "I'm not so sure it's the same thing," he said. "You were thirty, she is only seventeen." I failed to see how that made a difference, as the symptoms were all the same. Then he defended the psychiatrist, "She's better because of the medication," he told us.

I became exasperated. It was as if he was completely blind to what we had accomplished a few weeks earlier and deaf to everything I'd shared with him of my story. The next day, I put all of my key thoughts on paper, just to make sure that both parents were clear about where I stood. After that, it would be in God's hands.

As the weeks passed, our dreams of ending Ana's medication would fade. All of our efforts to convince her parents to let us work with her, free of meds, were rejected.

When her father informed Ligia that Ana would continue to listen to the psychiatrist, they fought and Ligia cried.

The next time I saw Ana, she was gone again, back to her old, smiling, insecure self. The argument between her father and Ligia had taken its toll. It wouldn't be long before Ana would enter into a depression.

Eventually, we heard back from Ana's parents. Based on the fact that Ana had experienced a manic episode which was followed by a depression, the psychiatrist informed them that she probably had bipolar disorder and would need to stay on medication for a minimum of two years. Ligia was furious and I was baffled. How is it that Ana's condition could look so much like my own, and yet require two years of medication? I became obsessed.

Night after night I scanned the Internet, checking websites, reading blogs, watching videos – all in the name of understanding what exactly is this thing called "bipolar disorder."

The more I discovered, the more concerned I became. It's a lifelong illness, like asthma or diabetes. It requires a lifetime of medication. The likelihood of a relapse into mania, once off medication, is around 90%. These medications have a never-ending list of brutal, long-term side effects – excessive weight gain, kidney failure, glaucoma, skin rashes, etc. Entire lives, once full of potential, are robbed of vitality forever.

However, upon closer scrutiny, the vast majority of the symptoms of bipolar mania were identical to the symptoms of a spiritual emergency. In fact, many of the people with bipolar disorder that I was reading about were having, basically, the same experience that I'd had ten years earlier.

It was as if I could hear alarm bells going off in my brain. These bipolar kids are having experiences of spiritual awakening, and they are being drugged for life!

Determined to get a thorough understanding, I dug into the work of some radical psychiatrists from the 1960s and '70s, Dr. R. D. Laing and Dr. John Weir Perry. Both claimed to be able to heal people with a more severe form of mental illness, schizophrenia.

I was shocked to discover that, on a sensory level, many people with schizophrenia were having the same set of experiences that I'd had: a feeling of oneness with everything; timelessness; thinking that you are a type of messiah, like Jesus; that you are on a mission from God; outpourings of love to almost anyone you feel good with; a confrontation with death; and violent rage when this experience is controlled or suppressed by parents, doctors or the police. In other words, at least on a sensory level, the experience of schizophrenia, bipolar mania or spiritual emergency could all be the same thing!

So why was I medication free while all of these people with bipolar disorder continued to relapse? I eventually reached the tentative hypothesis that bipolar mania is like a psycho-spiritual *vomiting* – a process that needs to continue until its completion or it will return again.

You see, one thing I learned from people with bipolar disorder online was that, in a typical situation, the manic person is confronted by the police or their family, who attempt to control them through physical force or verbal confrontation. In other words, they attempt to scare you into submission. In my case, I never allowed that to happen. Even when the police threatened to take me to jail, I ignored them. I refused to be manipulated. As a result, my process (my vomiting) was completed. For the vast majority, their manic process is "blocked" and that "block" is solidified with the medication. When the medication stops, the mania eventually returns. The manic process will never stop until it is complete. *All of the vomit needs to come out.* Since then, my opinion has been modified somewhat, but that was where I stood at the time.

With my research solidifying, I got more aggressive. I created a YouTube channel, bipolarORwakingUP, where I shared my own story through a series of videos. I figured that as long as the psychiatrist was telling Ana that she had a mental illness, I should be out there screaming the opposite. Not only did these videos help promote my newfound information; they also connected me with many people with bipolar disorder who completely related to my experience. As one girl said, "Sean, after hearing your story, I realized that my life could have been different. Thank you."

By listening to the stories of people from across the globe, I was able to better prepare myself for the task ahead.

My plan was simple – keep studying bipolar disorder until the psychiatrist informs the family that Ana will need medication for life. I was hoping they would find this out sooner rather than later, as side-effects were taking their toll. Ana was gaining weight very quickly. Then, with that dismal option in front of them, I would propose taking her off the meds, but with everyone's full knowledge that we will, most likely, need to take Ana through a full manic crisis once she is medication free.

Meanwhile, as I sifted through mountains of information, Ligia continued to work with Ana, encouraging her to widen her perspective, not only regarding her manic episode, but her life as well.

Even though she remained medicated, Ana made important strides toward creating a future that better reflected who she was as a person. Regular therapy sessions and yoga were an important part of this process, but probably most critical was that Ana made some very courageous decisions regarding her education.

Throughout high school, she had been groomed for a business related degree at the highly regarded University of São Paulo (USP), where her sister had studied. More than anything, it was the endless striving to get into USP which had led to Ana's depression, perhaps her entire disorder. Nevertheless, Ana was still taking a preparatory course to help her get into USP the following year. But as she revealed during her episode, it was not business that was in her heart, but nutrition.

Within a few weeks, Ana chose to finally quit the USP preparatory course and explore the possibility of taking a nutritional studies program at a school that better fit her own style. This represented an essential step in her development. It may not have healed her entirely, but it got her moving in the right direction. While Ana had no choice but to remain on mood stabilizers, she was off the anti-depressants soon after reaching her decision.

Love

The following July, Ana's sister, Eliana, returned from a six month university exchange in Paris. She had arrived in São Paulo aware of her sister's condition, hoping to help in any way she could. A week later, both Ana and Eliana paid us a visit, spending the night at our apartment.

Eliana was very excited from her journey, happy to be home, and planning on returning to USP that week. We spent the evening listening to stories of her adventures abroad, looking at photos. It was a great night. Interested in exploring education options here in the city, Ana had planned on staying with Eliana at her apartment for the rest of the week.

A few nights after their visit, Ligia got a phone call from Eliana.

"Sean, Eliana is all over the place. We've got to get over there," said Ligia, after hanging up.

I couldn't believe what I was hearing.

"Could Eliana be having a manic crisis too? *Exactly what soap opera am I living in?*" I thought.

When we arrived at her apartment, a few miles away, Eliana appeared agitated, but okay. She desperately wanted to share some ideas with Ligia that Ana found absurd and confusing.

Sitting at her dining room table, I remained quiet as the two of them went back and forth in Portuguese, speaking too fast for me to understand everything. Eliana was a little excited, but nothing too serious. Then she took us into her bedroom. There, written across her wall in large lipstick printing, was a poem in Portuguese,

> *"What is the World?*
> *The world cannot save itself,*
> *because it does not believe in itself.*
> *How can we love and be free at the same time?"*

"I wrote it down because it was important," she told us.

"I was crazy, but I never wrote on walls!" said Ana.

As the evening progressed, Eliana shared with us many new ideas, but she was having trouble expressing them clearly. However, I immediately understood where she was coming from. She was in an enlightened state.

"What is your experience of time?" I asked her.

"There is no time!" she said with a wide grin.

"It's this power, and with this power, you could control the world," she said.

"What is the power?" I asked.

"You can just read people. It's all there!"

I fondly recalled that power myself.

"This is going to happen to everybody!" she exclaimed.

"Why?" asked Ligia.

"Because we are already enlightened, we just don't know it," I answered.

"Yes! Yes!" Eliana shouted in excitement. She loved it when we could identify with her newfound insights.

At one point, I put a blanket over her shoulders as the three of us listened to her crazy wisdom. Whether she was making sense or not, was irrelevant. The point was that we were all there for her, all listening, without judgment.

"You are a real Buddha," I said. And she was, for the time being.

Eliana was relieved to be able to share her thoughts with us, and laid down to relax before I returned to our apartment. She was unable to sleep though, keeping Ligia up until 6:00 a.m. At her request, we didn't call her parents to let them know what was happening.

While I returned to work, Ligia stayed with the girls. However, during the next day, a tension started to build in the cramped apartment and Ligia came home as well. Eliana was reluctant to take our advice about staying safe in her apartment during this process, insisting that she go to some parties on the weekend. As she was with her sister, we let it be. Eliana was happy and was functioning adequately. But, as Ligia drove home, she felt her heart in her hands, leaving them alone to take care of themselves.

Friday night, while Ligia and I were watching television, I couldn't stop thinking about it, "We didn't protect her enough," I thought. "She's out there in São Paulo in a state of mania. Anything could happen." I was getting more worried by the minute.

At 12:30 a.m. we got the call, "I'm at a party and I'm scared."

Ligia and I got dressed and rushed over to pick her up as fast as we could.

"They'll have to run the ambulance right over me before she gets sent to the hospital," I told Ligia. I wasn't going to lose Eliana like I lost Ana. As Ligia drove through that infuriating maze known as São Paulo, I kept talking to Eliana on the cell phone.

"How did you do it Sean? How did you handle the fear?" she asked.

"You stay with people you love," I replied.

Upon entering the apartment complex, I shot straight up the stairwell to the second floor to find her alone in the dark. She was slumped over on the stairs, barefoot. Her cell phone, still activated, was lying on the floor. The moment the lights automatically turned on, she awoke, stood up to move toward me, then collapsed in my arms. I envisioned light-energy radiating out of my heart and into hers, so that she could regain consciousness. Ligia hugged her from behind. It seemed to work. After about a minute, she was back with us, barely.

We took her down to the car. Once on the street, Ligia said, "I've got to go back and get her shoes and purse." "Forget it!" I told her. "There will be time for that later."

On the way back to our apartment, she again collapsed in the elevator, this time on Ligia's shoulder. I picked her up and literally carried her through the door. Snapping back into her body, she screamed, in joyful hysteria, "I want to fly! I want to fly! I want to fly!" in her native Portuguese.

"She's a wild one!" I joked with Ligia. As serious as it was, we never lost our sense of humor regarding the absolute insanity of the situation.

Once inside, we immediately laid her down on our futon, situated in the "Zen-Bahia" space of our apartment – a place we use for relaxation and meditation. It's also our office.

"This is the shamanic process…. Enter the process…. Enter the shamanic process…," I whispered in Eliana's ear.

Within minutes she was shouting, "You were right! You were right!" as she rolled across the futon and then onto the floor. We quickly took the office chair, pottery, and anything else that might injure her out of the room. Ligia then brought in a few candles to emphasize the sacredness of the experience.

As Ligia stayed with her, she started to take off all of her clothes, shouting "Without shame! No more shame," repeatedly. Again, memories of my own experience returned. While Ligia and I couldn't help but smile, we let it all happen, as we believed it should. I remained respectful, staying out of the room. In fact, I went to get a synthetic fur blanket to cover her as she rolled about. Forcing her to get dressed was out of the question.

When I returned, she was darting around the room, insisting that she wanted to fly. Fulfilling my worst fears, she headed toward our glass balcony doors, trying to fly out of our thirteenth floor apartment.

"Sky! Sky!" she repeated again and again.

Seeing that Ligia was too small to handle the situation, I came into the room and stood in front of the sliding glass doors to our balcony. Eliana's torso bounced into my arm, and her foot banged into our computer desk as well. After that, she lay down again on the futon. I covered her with the blanket and then left her and Ligia in peace for a few minutes. Eliana was having a full blown, out-of-body experience – something far more intense than what I'd been through.

Watching from a short distance away, I saw her start to move and breathe in familiar patterns; deep, rapid breaths that led her into the darkest caverns of her psyche. With the blanket on top of her, she began gyrating her hips as if she were either having sex or giving birth. I recalled similar feelings during Breathwork sessions with Dr. Stan Grof years earlier, so I knew that she was going through some important work. Later, Eliana would explain that she was experiencing her own birth, that she felt as if she were in the womb again.

"Am I going to be in here for nine months?" was one of her passing thoughts.

Then the contractions started. With Ligia's support, she tightly contracted her abdomen as if a baby was about to arrive. After five long minutes of this, I came into the room to see if Ligia needed anything. When I moved toward them, Eliana asked for my hand and began to kiss it. She was in absolute ecstasy.

Ligia and Eliana slept in our bed that night while I slept on the futon. At some point during the night, Eliana fell off the bed on the way to the bathroom and hurt her foot. However, in the state she was in, she felt no pain.

As with most people in a bipolar manic episode, she didn't get much sleep. We went to bed at 6:00 a.m. and were up by about 10:30 a.m.

Concerned that Ana was alone in Eliana's São Paulo apartment, I went to pick her up. When we got back an hour later, Eliana was lying on the sofa with Ligia. During the day, Ligia, Ana and I took turns staying in physical contact with Eliana. As she lay there in an altered state, I would touch her back or her shoulder, as I remembered how much I needed a loving touch during my own experience. I can't imagine how disturbing it is to be one of the thousands of people out there who are locked up in isolation during an episode. Later, I was simply holding her left hand, maintaining a sacred state of mind. We would have sparse, but warm conversations.

At one point, she looked at me and said, "I need you."

"I need you too…. We need each other," I replied.

Then she turned on her stomach and looked me straight in the eyes.

"I believe in you," she said to me.

"I believe in you," she said again.

Nobody had ever spoken to me like that – no ego at all…just a pure spirit expressing her feelings.

"I believe in you too," I said. I kissed her on the forehead. She was a saint to me.

Her moods shifted during the day. At one point, she was crying a lot, so much so that she politely asked us all to leave the room. Later, while we were talking at the kitchen table, she asked if I believed in reincarnation. Apparently, death was on her mind.

Meals were certainly different, as I watched my once refined niece eat fried eggs with her bare hands. Upon finishing her meal, she was so exhausted that I needed to carry her back to bed.

Ligia also provided crayons for Eliana to express herself. "I'm free now," she told us, as she filled a page with the simple image of blue seagulls over open water.

Back on the couch, Eliana was "flying" again. I was perplexed, as I thought she was coming out of her altered states. Apparently, she had more work to do on the Other Side. Squirming around, she slid down onto the floor. Then, as I helped her back onto the couch, she started climbing up the back of it. I got nervous.

"What is she doing?"

She slithered away from me, as if trying to escape. I got up off the couch, losing touch-contact with her for the first time. Now she was standing on the back of the couch, balancing herself with her hands against the wall. Calmly shuffling in her direction, I circled around the side of the couch only to find that our leather foot-stool was blocking the distance between us.

"Uh-oh."

A second later, Eliana tried to leap over me and right through the glass balcony doors. Fortunately, she landed in my arms, letting out a primal scream along the way.

I don't remember that split second of my life. I have no mental image of her actually jumping.

For the first time, I was rattled. We all were.

"Well, I didn't see that coming," I told Ligia, as I carried Eliana back to the couch.

Lying down again, Eliana started to examine her arms. Unbeknownst to me, three days earlier she had bruised them by trying to walk through a wall after her yoga class.

"Where did these bruises come from?" she asked in a worrying tone. She felt the pain in her foot from when she had fallen out of bed the night before. "How did I hurt my foot?" She also noticed a bruised rib, probably from her jump.

"I don't know how these things happened, and I haven't felt any pain until now," she said. Her bliss was over. Now she was afraid.

"Look, I know you are trying to help me, but...I wasn't prepared for this.... Nobody is going to believe this," she said, in a worried tone.

"You've got that right!" I replied.

Recognizing her fear, but not knowing if she was in an altered state or not, Ligia tried to bring her back to reality.

"Okay, then let's bring you back. You are here! This is real!" she barked, banging on the dining room table.

"Is this a hospital?" Eliana asked, staring ominously at our white walls.

"No, this is our apartment and you are okay," I said.

"Am I dying?"

"In a way, but you will be okay."

"Was I selling drugs in Europe?"

"No."

We answered her questions as best we could, trying to alleviate her fears, but it was of little use. Exhausted, I finally asked her, "What are you afraid of?"

"I'm afraid of you."

At that point I knew it was my time to step away. Eliana had associated me so completely with the other level of reality that, while she was there, in bliss, I was her hero. Now that she was afraid, I was somehow to blame. At least that's what I thought was happening. Ligia took control of things for the rest of the night while I got some rest.

Later that night, four days into the episode, Ligia contacted Eliana's mother, Maria, for the first time. On the phone with her mother, I overheard Eliana say, "No, Sean's not here. He's afraid of me."

Even though I knew her feelings toward me would change again, it still hurt. I went to bed feeling somewhat defeated. I prayed that night, "God, Ligia and I are wiped out. Please help Eliana get some sleep and come back to reality. I think she's done."

Unable to sleep, I moved to the couch in front of the futon, where Eliana slept with her sister. I did so because I was scared to death that Eliana would make another move for the balcony. Every noise I heard that night sounded like those glass doors opening. I fell asleep around 5:30 a.m. The girls slept through the whole night.

The next morning, Ligia jumped in bed with the girls for a friendly wake up call. I could hear them laughing. I crept in, sneaking up to Eliana's face to take a peek. She broke out in a big laugh. She was back!

The Eliana that returned was sane, but not entirely the girl we knew. A little angry and very sensitive, she wanted to be left alone. She was suffering for reasons we weren't entirely sure of. Later that day, we dropped her off with Ana at their parents' home.

Sitting down with Maria, I tried my best to explain what had to take place.

"Patience, patience…" I begged. "She's okay, she just needs some time."

I said what needed to be said, but after our experience with Ana, I knew that my efforts were futile. In order to "help" their daughter, they were going to do the exact opposite.

"I know you don't believe me," I told Maria.

She held my hand compassionately, "I believe that it's your interpretation."

"My interpretation…my interpretation…" I murmured to myself in frustration.

"Ten years…ten years of trying to explain myself and still nobody gets it! It doesn't matter what I say or do, nobody understands!" I thought.

By this point, Eliana was eager to see us go. With our nerves frayed to the edges, even Ligia and I got short with each other. It was not the Hollywood ending that I'd hoped for.

However, as we drove home I felt certain that, if we had to do everything all over again, I wouldn't change a thing. We gave Eliana everything we had for five straight days. I think that's all anyone could ask for.

The next day, Ligia dealt with the stress of the weekend by heading straight back to her English classes, as they helped her forget the chaos we'd just been through. She also went to the park to cleanse herself with her own rituals.

As for me, I cancelled my entire teaching schedule and stayed in bed the whole day. The experience was just too overwhelming. On the one hand, I wasn't sure if Eliana would be able to survive the amount of bullshit that was about to come her way. I was scared for her. But on the other, I knew that Ligia and I had just done something remarkable, taking a completely unprepared person through a manic experience without doctors or hospitalization. As dangerous as it had been, I was proud of all of us, especially Eliana.

The experience also gave meaning to everything that I'd been through. Finally, here was something that felt like the spiritual work I'd been searching for since my hospitalization. For the first time in my life, I had a voice speaking to me, saying, "This is who I am, this is what I do." This was the work of a true shaman.

HOPE

Eliana's first few weeks at home were terrible. As expected, her parents were doing everything normal parents do, not realizing that they were only making things worse. In the first week, they took her to two local psychologists and her sister's psychiatrist, all against our recommendations. We had asked for patience. Instead, they hit the panic button.

Thankfully, because we had allowed her to work through her process, the psychiatrist was unable to detect any manic symptoms and let her walk away, medication free. I couldn't believe it. Apparently, she was smart enough to keep her mouth shut in front of the doctor. But, this didn't mean that all was well beneath the surface.

"You're controlling me, you're controlling me!" was her mantra during these first few weeks at home. Apparently, Eliana felt controlled by her parents at even the slightest suggestion from them. For the first time in her life, she was arguing with them daily.

As living with them became too confrontational, Eliana chose to stay at her apartment in São Paulo as much as her parents would allow. Maria usually insisted on staying with her most nights, as even she realized that the tension between Eliana and her father was too much for the family to bear.

While Eliana was having problems at home, she wasn't exactly eager to listen to us, either. Despite repeatedly suggesting that she slow down and relax, she chose to fill her schedule with activities, returning to her normal life as if nothing had ever happened.

Meeting us for lunch about a month later, she was a bit uncomfortable talking about what had happened. Although she could see the value of her experience and was grateful not to be medicated, she wasn't doing much to integrate the experience into her daily life. The one exception was that she had started seeing her new therapist, a transpersonal psychologist whom Ligia had sought out and wisely recommended.

Then, just days after our lunch together, Eliana had a relapse. She had been studying too much and was unable to sleep for three days. That, along with some nearby construction noise and the typical chaos of São Paulo, led to her entering a state of confusion.

Reaching out for comfort and reassurance, she called her mother. But, by this point, Maria wasn't risking anything. Despite Eliana's insistence that she was "fine," her parents drove down from their city of Itu to pick her up. Once in the hands of her parents, she was on the phone to us as soon as she could.

"They're forcing me to take drugs," she told me. Once again, they had dragged her to the psychiatrist.

"I'm sorry, Eliana," I said, feeling defeated once more.

"It's okay," she replied.

"I believe in you, Eliana," I told her. That was about the extent of our conversation.

"You're killing me, you know that," she repeatedly told her parents. "Is that what you want?"

In the end, she agreed to take medication for ten days.

To my astonishment, Maria visited us a week later. She was frustrated and looking for help. Apparently, all of Ligia's efforts and my conversations with her were finally paying off. As it turns out, Maria had been reading much of the Portuguese material that Ligia had given her. While none of it had convinced Maria with total certainty that Eliana did not have the chemical imbalance that psychiatry said she had, the books did widen her eyes to alternative perspectives.

Through our recommended reading, Maria was introduced to theories of mental illness brought forth not only by Dr. Stanislav Grof, but also Dr. Roberto Assagioli, Dr. Carl Jung, Ken Wilber and others. Maria contrasted this mix of somewhat optimistic opinions with the hopeless certainty of their current psychiatrist, and realized that there might be something to what we had been saying.

"Eliana is not integrating, she's not dealing with her experience," she told us. As Eliana was coming off the medication the following day, Maria didn't know what to do.

I was quick to offer a suggestion. Going back to my "vomit theory" I said, "Well, the first time Eliana was with us she got a lot out, but obviously she had more to go. Then, the second episode was blocked by you guys and the medications, correct?" Maria nodded in agreement.

"If she is coming off the meds tomorrow, I think it's highly likely that she will relapse within two weeks, to get it all out – whuaaah!" I said, imitating vomit noises. "When that happens, call us and we will work her through it together."

Maria was open and listening, but she didn't really want to hear it. The idea of a third episode was not something that she looked forward to, nor did Ligia or Eliana. But I wanted it. I wanted to see us all work together, both sides of the family. I wanted to see Eliana heal completely, as I knew she could. And, selfishly, I wanted to spend a few more hours with that pure, unshackled spirit.

Before she left our apartment, I said to Maria, "I just want to thank you for considering our ideas. I know they are very different for you."

"To be honest, you simply offer a more hopeful perspective than what the doctors are saying," she said.

That's when it hit me. For parents, it's not about my experience, my education on the subject, or the soundness of the theory. It's not that at all. It's about results. They want their daughter back, and if they need to go to a Mongolian shaman or a German neurosurgeon, that is exactly what they will do.

Soon after Maria boarded the elevator, I sat on the futon to digest what had just transpired. A vision passed my mind of the Earth's tectonic plates shifting dramatically. After enduring months of frustration, fighting against the mainstream opinions and quick-fix solutions of psychiatry, the game had suddenly turned in our favor.

Eliana's third episode started two weeks later, right on schedule. With her energy level on the rise, Ligia would stay with Maria and Eliana at her apartment. A few days later, Eliana went into a rebirthing process right in the middle of her therapy session. Ligia called me with the news and we made plans for Eliana, Maria, Ligia and me to sleep at the psychologist's clinic overnight (only in Brazil!).

"Do you want to come over?" Eliana asked, over the phone. She sounded like she was inviting me to a party.

"I see elephants!" she giggled.

After picking up some supplies for our little camp-out, I arrived at the clinic around midnight. Eliana looked weary, but positively radiant. Not wanting to disturb the sacred mood which had developed, I entered quietly.

At first she was quite groggy, but she livened up as I sat down. Most of her conversation was only half crazy, so I wasn't worried at all. Apparently, she had been keeping herself occupied by repainting the psychologist's wall art with dried banana chips. I was pleasantly surprised to discover that she actually was seeing elephants, as the clinic was decorated with images of the Hindu god, Ganesh and other pachyderms.

At one point, I brought a box of matches into the room to light some candles for one last, sacred evening together. Catching me off-guard, Eliana snatched the box of matches from my hand, lit one and held it up in front of her face.

Looking back, I can see how, rationally, the right thing to do would have been to blow out that match, as she was sitting across from me on the floor. It would have been easy. It also would have been a mistake.

I was not sitting across from a young woman now. I was sitting across from a jaguar. A jaguar that was testing me, and any sign of fear could have meant a serious problem. Facing her, I shifted up onto my hands and knees, moving my nose within inches of the match. Through the flame, I calmly stared into her eyes, letting her know that I was ready for anything – one jaguar to another. With that, she blew out the match, sending the sulfur smoke into my face.

Ligia brought four candles to where we were planning on sleeping, in the middle of the clinic's den. As we lit the candles, I named them after each of us, "Eliana…Ligia… Maria…Sean!" Eliana laughed at our new symbol of solidarity.

As we prepared to go to sleep that night, Eliana reached out for me to hold her hand. I lay down beside her and she turned, so that we would have been spooning if we had been in bodily contact. I held her hand with my right, and laid my left hand on her left shoulder. After helping Maria get settled, Ligia came in and put a blanket over the two of us. I would stay awake with Eliana for almost the entire night, protecting her and sending her love. Despite trying to get some sleep, Ligia would lie across from us, awake, until sunrise.

As dawn approached, I fell asleep and Ligia moved Eliana into another room because I was snoring (getting old, I guess). She slept like a rock until about noon. As for me, I went to work before she woke up.

Walking me out to the car, Ligia asked, "Do you think she'll have another relapse?"

"I don't think so," I said.

"Tonight was perfect.... Both sides of the family working together.... The right location.... Her experience was totally unblocked. There was an art to the whole thing. It was perfect."

Ligia and I had a warm hug on the curb, chatting with the same mutual admiration and vitality that had carried us through our first eight years together.

Predictably, Eliana returned to this "reality" overly sensitive, weak and tired. For the first week or so she remained frustrated at her inability to concentrate on reading, studying, etc. However, as she got used to her new Self, she was able to return to university, completing her semester, passing all of her exams, medication free – a remarkable achievement.

Meeting her for lunch before the Christmas holidays, we talked about some of the details of her experience. This time, she was able to look back on the whole thing with objective eyes.

"Do you think you might have a relapse?" I asked her.

"I don't think so," she said. "After the first two episodes I was sort of in denial, acting like I was fine and everything was okay. But then during the third one it was like...*I give up.*"

"Ahhhh, the surrender!" I said, happy with her answer.

As we continued our conversation, I provided a few helpful hints for the future.

"Pay attention to your dreams," I said. "They can help you understand yourself and provide direction in your life."

"And watch for the synchronicities. If you find yourself in a surprising situation, pay close attention. There could be meaning in it for you," I suggested.

As an example, I told her about the dream I had with Charles Lindbergh's plane, *The Spirit of St. Louis*, which I mentioned in Part 1. As with most young Brazilians, she had never heard of him before.

The next day, I met Eliana again at Ana's birthday party in Itu. We had dinner together with the whole family.

"Guess who my history professor was talking about in class this morning?" she asked, rhetorically. "Charles Lindberg!"

"I love that!" I told her. "It lets me know I'm in the Zone!"

Leaving the restaurant that night, Eliana's father came over and quietly thanked me for everything we had done.

While the exam period was understandably stressful, by the holidays, Eliana was positively mellow. Even her younger cousin noticed the difference, aptly nicknaming her "Eli-Zen."

Looking at her now, I see myself ten years ago – calmer, more open, receptive and passionate; knowing eyes, faith in life, *a quiet mind*.

I can't wait to see her when she's thirty.

FAITH

I wish I could end our story by saying that we were able to take Ana off her meds as well. In fact, without informing anyone, she tried it herself, stopping her medication just before her eighteenth birthday, in December of 2007.

Despite being bothered by her decision to act without talking to us first, we chose to be supportive once she was meds free. Besides, on a personal level, her life had improved a great deal since the time of her crisis, nine months earlier. She had recently been accepted into an excellent nutritional studies program, something she was very proud of. Plus, she was doing therapy, yoga and volunteer work on a regular basis. Ligia and Maria thought there was a good possibility that she may not relapse at all. Personally, I estimated her chances of success at about 50/50.

The timing of her relapse could not have been worse. It happened while I was in Canada for the Christmas holidays and, unlike her first episode, she was violent and uncooperative, even with Ligia. Despite the entire family doing their best to show patience with her, after being in a manic state for nine days, Ana needed to be hospitalized.

Ironically, if she had been violent in her first episode we never would have gotten involved in her situation at all. According to Dr. Grof, violent and uncooperative behavior is indicative of mental illness, not spiritual emergency.[1]

So what changed?

I suspected that the medications had a detrimental effect. After her relapse, I searched for information on the link between violence and her medication, Depakote. While I was able to find research connecting other medications such as neuropleptics[2], lithium[3] and anti-depressants[4] to violent behavior, condemning research on mood stabilizers like Depakote remained elusive. Then, a year later in December, 2008 the FDA insisted that Depakote come with a suicide warning within its packaging.

Too little, too late.

If I had been aware of the profound psychological hazards of this medication at the time, perhaps we could have been better prepared.

Nevertheless, I remain optimistic. About a month out of the hospital, Ana called Ligia to share a story. Apparently, she had been getting a massage to help her relax after her recent relapse. Lying on the table in the therapist's clinic, she experienced a hallucination – a giant conch shell floating in the corner. Later, the shell moved to in front of Ana's heart.

After her massage, she told the masseuse what she had seen. To Ana's surprise, the masseuse had a statue of Yemanjá, the Brazilian *goddess of the sea*, tucked away in the back of her clinic. The therapist was a worshipper of this particular goddess.

"Ahhh, she's still out there..." I told Ligia.

For me, Ana's vision was a sign. Somehow, despite the fact that I would have loved to help her work through her process, everything was *as it should be.*

Ana's story reminded me of one final vision from my own hospitalization, which I have yet to share.

Restrained to the bed with my father's hand on my back, I saw a reddish brown fox at the edge of a snowy forest in my mind's eye. Darting back and forth at the tree line, his movements seemed to make no sense at all.

"God is crazy," I mumbled to myself with a smile. "Crazy like a fox!"

Of course, the fox knew exactly what he was doing. He was trying to catch a sheep in the distance. As opposed to chasing after one directly, he'd learned to first confuse the flock by running from one side to the other. Then he went in for the kill. In truth, the fox was not crazy at all – he was operating on a whole other level.

As scary, frustrating and confusing as life can be sometimes, I've learned that it's best to simply surrender to God's will and forget about your own plans. Because, while life may look like utter madness, there is always a sublime love hidden beneath all the drama – a love which brings tears to my eyes. Living in the light of a God like that, how can we not have faith?

***

EPILOGUE

Over a decade ago, I first wrote down the events surrounding my hospitalization and sent them to that "envious" transpersonal psychologist I mentioned in Part 1. In that document, I wrote the following concluding comments:

May, 1998

Travelling Peru, our guide, Dr. Alberto Villoldo, spoke of how the shaman lives in the world of percept, as opposed to precept. Of any shamanic practice, that is the one I've come closest to mastering.

After returning to Toronto, I was unsure if I wanted to "engrave in stone" my memories of what happened during my hospitalization of the previous year. I could see quite clearly that I do have a choice as to how I wish to remember the experience.

Do I choose to remember myself as the victim of a weekend program that refuses to take responsibility for their course members if they begin to act strangely? Do I choose to recall incompetent psychiatrists who seek to control rather than heal patients? Do I choose to remember myself as someone who completely embarrassed himself, acting like an idiot in a downtown hotel?

Or do I choose to see everyone, including myself, doing the best they can, given the circumstances? Do I choose to accept a once in a lifetime gift that is beyond my comprehension?

And how will this past effect my future?

Will I allow it to be a dark secret that I dare not share with co-workers? Do I try to put the experience behind me so that I may strive to piece together that ever elusive "normal" life we are all supposed to aspire to? Or do I celebrate the episode as a divine rebirth, the hell with what the masses say?

The choice is mine. I am in charge of how I interpret my reality. I am in charge of how I will help create my future.

I choose to believe that the entire sequence of events described here was a crucial part of a destiny that I can feel inside of me, but still cannot clearly see or name.

Be it "fantasy" or "reality," I know in my heart that I looked death in the face and embraced it in a spirit of divine surrender. Nobody can take that away from me. My life has never been the same since.

Fast-forwarding to the present, it is much clearer to me how naturally and deliberately the events of my life have unfolded. In the past, I've often felt as if I were a blind mouse, navigating the maze of life solely on intuition. On many occasions I never knew why I needed to do something, or go somewhere – I just knew I had to.

In retrospect, it's easy to trace how the prophetic dreams, synchronicities and visionary experiences that I've shared here have been the pivotal events of what has been a remarkably satisfying journey. "Destroying my life" in advertising, while slow and painful, was the most important decision I ever made. Discovering the role I have to play as a shamanic guide and advocate to a whole bipolar generation has been a startling revelation. As for becoming a writer, let's just say that the experience of sharing my story with you has already been a reward in itself.

Guiding Eliana through her process was the single most important experience of my life; for the first time shedding light on the intense, winding path I've been asked to follow. For almost two decades I wondered why it was so difficult for me to find a satisfying career. It was only with this experience that I could clearly understand. Finally, here was something of tangible benefit to others – the spiritual rebirth of a member of my own Brazilian family.

The challenge now, of course, is to do whatever I can to help others through this extraordinary, yet difficult process. For people under the age of twenty-one, diagnosis of bipolar disorder rose 4000% between 1994 and 2003.[1] The vast majority of these people are being told by their psychiatrist that they have a permanent chemical imbalance which will require medication for their entire lives. Now, it may be true that there will always be some people who will require medications, perhaps forever, but I hope that one day meds are considered more as a helpful tool than as a permanent way of life.

In a way, our work with Ana and Eliana has confirmed my deepest suspicions about myself. I probably won't be around to see the "Heaven on Earth" that felt so close during my own episode; but that's fine because, honestly, I don't feel that I was born for a truly blissful life. I haven't earned it yet.

No, my job is to do battle, to "pave the road" so the purer, more sensitive souls can survive their awakenings. I find myself in an ideal situation for helping people from across the globe learn to take back and validate what once had the potential to be the most sacred experience of their lives; one that our entire society has violently stripped away from them out of fear and ignorance.

The biggest part of that "paving" process is to raise awareness of the spiritually healing potential of bipolar disorder, a huge part of which involves my YouTube channel, bipolarORwakingUP.

While the number of views my videos receive pales in comparison to that of a cat playing piano, the lives I've touched, not only with my story, but with my theory videos as well, are among the first baby-steps toward our entire world looking at bipolar disorder in a revolutionary, new way. Receiving enthusiastic e-mails and comments from people in Australia, Bulgaria, France, India, Norway, Saudi Arabia, Uruguay, etc., it certainly looks like the whole world is waking up!

To know that, in some small way, I'm helping them understand, validate and accept their experiences means more to me than anything I ever did in advertising. Like I tell Ligia, "YouTube is the best job I've ever had, even though the pay sucks!"

Along with the videos, we are also "walking our talk," helping a few brave pioneers out there work through their episodes without meds or hospitalization. As Ligia and I gain more experience, we are improving our approach to this process, trying to create a safe and sacred atmosphere which will permit the person in crisis to work through his or her spiritual awakening unencumbered. It's safe to say we won't be working in our thirteenth floor apartment again.

With that said, I am fully aware of the challenges which confront our work. The very idea of bipolar disorder being a natural mechanism which is intended to heal through a form of spiritual awakening is, well, heretical, to say the least. Our work is a serious challenge, not only to psychiatry, but also to mainstream Freudian psychology which views all forms of direct spiritual experience as a sign of pathology.

The notion that God is a factual entity which can be experienced directly by anyone through what has been commonly referred to as a "manic episode" or "acute psychosis" calls into question the fundamental tenets of both modern science and its historical rival, religion. If the material world is not as "real" as we first imagined, but actually the offspring of a limitless spiritual plane, where does that leave science? If God already exists in the hearts of all mankind, expressing his divinity as an experience of perfect, unconditional love, how can any religion claim to be the one true faith?

One of the joys of being in touch with people from around the world has been to verify that this divine encounter has been experienced by Christians of many denominations, Jews, Muslims, those who follow Buddhist practices and even atheists! Of course, there are no atheists afterwards.

The corporate world will not exactly be thrilled with our new approach to mental illness either. How long will any of us stay chained to our cubicles after we have been blessed by the arrival of the Great Awakening? Let's face it, enlightenment is bad for business. Anyone who thinks that Big Pharma and psychiatry will be thrilled with the "discovery" that bipolar disorder is ideally treated without a lifetime supply of expensive medications is painfully naïve.

However, as time passes and people start talking, I'm sure that thousands, if not millions will begin to come through their manic experiences feeling reborn, as Eliana, myself, and a few others already have. Once it becomes common knowledge that bipolar disorder does not necessarily lead to a life of "meds, death or insanity" as psychiatry would have us believe, we're in a whole new ballgame.

THANK YOU

To the woman who changed my life forever, my wife, Ligia. You have been my best friend, mentor, lover, therapist and playmate since we met. You are always the first person to stand up for me, and the only one on the planet who can keep me from bullshitting myself. Without you, my life doesn't even happen. Your intuitive knowing of what "sings" and what "sinks" has been of enormous help in telling my story. That face never lies.

To Mom and Dad, for your love and support on a journey that would be difficult for any parent to understand. Thank you for always being there for me – no matter what!

To Sheena, for years you've been listening to me, listening…never offering an answer; always presenting the right question. It may not have been therapy, but it sure helped! Your faith in life has always been an inspiration.

To everyone in the online bipolar community who has shared their experiences with me. Most of what I have learned about this "disorder" has come, not from doctors or books, but from you. You have all been great teachers! One day, your contributions will reap huge dividends.

Special thanks to my team of helpful proofreaders, Michael Pearson, Hank Cotrim, Elizabeth Wolf and Ligia. Your contribution has been invaluable.

And finally, to my two wonderful Brazilian nieces, "Ana" and "Eliana". You are the motivation and inspiration for this book, my YouTube videos, and everything else that Ligia and I do with regard to bipolar disorder. Thank you for allowing me to share our stories together, and for having faith in us.

notes

Part 1

1. *Joseph Campbell and the Power of Myth*, with Bill Moyers, (PBS, 1988). Now available on DVD.
2. James Redfield, *The Celestine Prophesy*, (Wheeler Publishing, 1994).
3. C. G. Jung, *Memories, Dreams, Reflections*, (Vintage Books, 1989).
4. Lao Tsu, *Tao Te Ching* (Barnes & Noble Inc., 1993) and, Deng Ming Dao, *Chronicles of Tao*, (HarperCollins Publishers, 1993).
5. John G. Neihardt, *Black Elk Speaks*, (Bison Books, 2004).

Part 2

1. Paramahansa Yogananda, *Autobiography of a Yogi* (Self-Realization Fellowship, 1998).
2. Sogyal Rinpoche, *The Tibetan Book of Living and Dying*, (HarperSanFrancisco, 1994), 330.
3. Christina and Stanislav Grof, M.D., *The Stormy Search for the Self*, (G. P. Putnam's Sons, 1992), 73-77.
4. Ibid., 1-7.
5. Ibid., 88.
6. M. J. Abadie, *Your Psychic Potential*, (Adams Media Corporation, 1995), 108-109.
7. Ibid., 150-153.
8. Ibid., 159.
9. Alberto Villoldo, *Dance of the Four Winds*, and *Island of the Sun,* (Destiny Books, 1995).

Part 3

1. Christina and Stanislav Grof, M.D., *The Stormy Search for the Self*, 254-255.

2. Robert Whitaker, *Mad in America*, (Basic Books), 188-189.

3. Ibid., 248-249.

4. See www.ssristories.com for an account of anti-depressant related murder and suicide.

Epilogue

1. Benedict Carey, "Bipolar Illness Soars as Diagnosis for the Young," New York Times, September 4, 2007.

LINKS

Any online activities or channels that I am involved with such as YouTube, Facebook, Twitter, NING, etc., can be accessed from my central website at:

www.bipolarORwakingUP.com

Printed in Great Britain
by Amazon